Getting Value Out of Value-Added

REPORT OF A WORKSHOP

Committee on Value-Added Methodology for Instructional Improvement,
Program Evaluation, and Educational Accountability

Henry Braun, Naomi Chudowsky, and Judith Koenig, *Editors*

Center for Education

Division of Behavioral and Social Sciences and Education

NATIONAL RESEARCH COUNCIL *and* NATIONAL ACADEMY OF EDUCATION

THE NATIONAL ACADEMIES PRESS
Washington, D.C.
www.nap.edu

THE NATIONAL ACADEMIES PRESS   500 Fifth Street, N.W.   Washington, DC 20001

NOTICE: The project that is the subject of this report was approved by the Governing Board of the National Research Council, whose members are drawn from the councils of the National Academy of Sciences, the National Academy of Engineering, and the Institute of Medicine. The members of the committee responsible for the report were chosen for their special competences and with regard for appropriate balance.

This study was supported by Award No. B 8204 between the National Academy of Sciences and Carnegie Corporation of New York. Any opinions, findings, conclusions, or recommendations expressed in this publication are those of the author(s) and do not necessarily reflect the views of the organizations or agencies that provided support for the project.

International Standard Book Number-13:   978-0-309-14813-9
International Standard Book Number-10:   0-309-14813-8

Additional copies of this report are available from National Academies Press, 500 Fifth Street, N.W., Lockbox 285, Washington, DC 20055; (800) 624-6242 or (202) 334-3313 (in the Washington metropolitan area); Internet, http://www.nap.edu.

Suggested citation: National Research Council and National Academy of Education. (2010). *Getting Value Out of Value-Added: Report of a Workshop*. Committee on Value-Added Methodology for Instructional Improvement, Program Evaluation, and Educational Accountability, Henry Braun, Naomi Chudowsky, and Judith Koenig, Editors. Center for Education, Division of Behavioral and Social Sciences and Education. Washington, DC: The National Academies Press.

THE NATIONAL ACADEMIES
Advisers to the Nation on Science, Engineering, and Medicine

The **National Academy of Sciences** is a private, nonprofit, self-perpetuating society of distinguished scholars engaged in scientific and engineering research, dedicated to the furtherance of science and technology and to their use for the general welfare. Upon the authority of the charter granted to it by the Congress in 1863, the Academy has a mandate that requires it to advise the federal government on scientific and technical matters. Dr. Ralph J. Cicerone is president of the National Academy of Sciences.

The **National Academy of Engineering** was established in 1964, under the charter of the National Academy of Sciences, as a parallel organization of outstanding engineers. It is autonomous in its administration and in the selection of its members, sharing with the National Academy of Sciences the responsibility for advising the federal government. The National Academy of Engineering also sponsors engineering programs aimed at meeting national needs, encourages education and research, and recognizes the superior achievements of engineers. Dr. Charles M. Vest is president of the National Academy of Engineering.

The **Institute of Medicine** was established in 1970 by the National Academy of Sciences to secure the services of eminent members of appropriate professions in the examination of policy matters pertaining to the health of the public. The Institute acts under the responsibility given to the National Academy of Sciences by its congressional charter to be an adviser to the federal government and, upon its own initiative, to identify issues of medical care, research, and education. Dr. Harvey V. Fineberg is president of the Institute of Medicine.

The **National Research Council** was organized by the National Academy of Sciences in 1916 to associate the broad community of science and technology with the Academy's purposes of furthering knowledge and advising the federal government. Functioning in accordance with general policies determined by the Academy, the Council has become the principal operating agency of both the National Academy of Sciences and the National Academy of Engineering in providing services to the government, the public, and the scientific and engineering communities. The Council is administered jointly by both Academies and the Institute of Medicine. Dr. Ralph J. Cicerone and Dr. Charles M. Vest are chair and vice chair, respectively, of the National Research Council.

www.national-academies.org

Preface

BACKGROUND

Value-added methods refer to efforts to estimate the relative contributions of specific teachers, schools, or programs to student test performance. In recent years, these methods have attracted considerable attention because of their potential applicability for educational accountability, teacher pay-for-performance systems, school and teacher improvement, program evaluation, and research. Value-added methods involve complex statistical models applied to test data of varying quality. Accordingly, there are many technical challenges to ascertaining the degree to which the output of these models provides the desired estimates. Despite a substantial amount of research over the last decade and a half, overcoming these challenges has proven to be very difficult, and many questions remain unanswered—at a time when there is strong interest in implementing value-added models in a variety of settings.

In 2005 the National Research Council (NRC) and the National Academy of Education decided to jointly plan a workshop to help identify areas of emerging consensus and areas of disagreement regarding appropriate uses of value-added methods, in an effort to provide research-based guidance to policy makers who are facing decisions about whether to proceed in this direction. The project was funded by the Carnegie Corporation. A steering committee was formed to plan the event, facilitate the workshop discussions, and oversee the writing of the report. The committee members were chosen for their expertise in educational testing and accountability, valued-added methodology from both the economics and statistical traditions, and state and local data systems.

The Workshop on Valued-Added Methodology for Instructional Improvement, Program Evaluation, and Educational Accountability was held on November 13 and 14, 2008, in Washington, DC. The workshop agenda and a list of participants are in Appendix A. Biographical sketches of committee members and staff appear in Appendix B. The background papers and workshop transcript are posted on the NRC website at http://www7.nationalacademies.org/bota/VAM_Workshop_Agenda.html.

This report is a summary of discussions at the workshop. It should be noted that the report summarizes the views expressed by workshop participants. While the committee is responsible for the overall quality and accuracy of the report as a record of what transpired at the workshop, the views contained in the workshop report are not necessarily those of the committee.

Acknowledgments

Many people contributed to the success of this project. We would first like to thank the members of the National Academy of Education's Research Advisory Committee, who helped to formulate the project. They include Alan Schoenfeld, University of California, who chairs the group; Richard Atkinson, University of California; James Banks, University of Washington; Margaret Eisenhart, University of Colorado at Boulder; Michael Feuer, National Research Council; Robert Hauser, University of Wisconsin–Madison; Ellen Lagemann, Bard College; Michael McPherson, Spencer Foundation; Lauren Resnick, University of Pittsburgh; Lorrie Shepard, University of Colorado at Boulder; and Marshall Smith, William and Flora Hewlett Foundation. We would also like to thank Laura Desimone, University of Pennsylvania, who assisted in development of a concept proposal on value-added methods. The committee is also indebted to Gregory White, executive director, and Andrea Solarz, director of research initiatives, at the National Academy of Education, for their helpful suggestions throughout the course of this project.

We are also grateful to senior staff members of the National Research Council's (NRC's) Division of Behavioral and Social Sciences and Education who helped to move this project forward. Michael Feuer, executive director, and Patricia Morison, associate executive director and acting director of the Center for Education, provided support and guidance at key stages in this project. Eugenia Grohman, associate executive director, and Kirsten Sampson Snyder, senior report review officer, offered their knowledge and experience with NRC procedures to guide the report through the NRC review process. Christine McShane, senior editor, provided expert editing assistance.

The committee also recognizes the scholars who wrote papers for the workshop. These individuals provided the intellectual foundations for the report: Dale Ballou, Vanderbilt University; Derek Briggs, University of Colorado at Boulder; John Easton, University of Chicago; Adam Gamoran, University of Wisconsin–Madison; Robert Gordon, Center for American Progress; Ben Jensen, Organisation for Economic Co-operation and Development; Ashish Jha, Harvard School of Public Health; Michael Kane, National Conference of Bar Examiners; Michael Kolen, University of Iowa; Helen Ladd, Duke University; Robert Linn, University of Colorado at Boulder; J.R. Lockwood and Dan McCaffrey, RAND Corporation; Sean Reardon, Stanford University; and Mark Reckase, Michigan State University.

The committee also thanks the NRC staff who worked directly on this project. We are grateful to Stuart Elliott, director, and Judith Koenig, senior program officer, of the Board on Testing and Assessment for their contributions in formulating the workshop design and making it a reality. We particularly wish to recognize Naomi Chudowsky, costudy director of the project. Naomi took the lead in translating workshop discussions into a draft report. She then helped to prepare successive versions of the report for committee review, deftly and diplomatically handling numerous and diverse committee comments.

Finally, as chair of the committee, I wish to thank the committee members for their dedication and outstanding contributions to this project. They actively assisted in all stages of this project, from planning the workshop and identifying presenters, to reviewing multiple versions of this report. They gave generously of their time to ensure that the final product accurately represents the workshop discussions, is understandable to a variety of audiences, and fully portrays the complex issues associated with value-added methods.

This report has been reviewed in draft form by individuals chosen for their diverse perspectives and technical expertise, in accordance with procedures approved by the NRC's Report Review Committee. The purpose of this independent review is to provide candid and critical comments that will assist the institution in making the published report as sound as possible and to ensure that the report meets institutional standards for objectivity, evidence, and responsiveness to the study charge. The review comments and draft manuscript remain confidential to protect the integrity of the deliberative process.

We wish to thank the following people for their review of this report: Duncan Chaplin, Human Services Research Division, Mathematica Policy Research, Inc.; Mark Dynarski, Center for Improving Research Evidence,

Mathematica Policy Research, Inc.; Drew H. Gitomer, Policy Evaluation and Research Center, Educational Testing Service; Maciej Jakubowski, Directorate for Education, Indicators and Analysis Division, Programme for International Student Assessment, Organisation for Economic Co-operation and Development; Sean F. Reardon, School of Education, Stanford University; and Paul R. Sackett, Department of Psychology, University of Minnesota.

Although the reviewers listed above have provided many constructive comments and suggestions, they were not asked to endorse the content of the report, nor did they see the final draft of the report before its release. The review of this report was overseen by Paul Sackett, University of Minnesota. Appointed by the NRC, he was responsible for making certain that an independent examination of this report was carried out in accordance with institutional procedures and that all review comments were carefully considered. Responsibility for the final content of this report rests entirely with the authoring committee and the institution.

Henry Braun, *Chair*
Committee on Value-Added Methodology
for Instructional Improvement, Program
Evaluation, and Educational Accountability

Contents

1

Introduction to Value-Added Modeling

In the context of education, value-added methodology refers to efforts to measure the effects on the achievement of students of their current teachers, schools, or educational programs,[1] taking account of the differences in prior achievement and (perhaps) other measured characteristics that students bring with them to school. In this report, we use the term "value-added models" to refer to a variety of sophisticated statistical techniques that use one or more years of prior student test scores, as well as other data, to adjust for preexisting differences among students when calculating contributions to student test performance.

Value-added models have attracted considerable attention in recent years. They have obvious appeal to those interested in teacher and school accountability, instructional improvement, program evaluation, or education research. The No Child Left Behind Act of 2001 (NCLB) requires all states to test students annually in grades 3-8 and in one grade in high school, and this growing availability of student achievement data has led to greater opportunities to implement these models. At the same time, however, many researchers have questioned the validity of the inferences drawn from value-added models in view of the many technical challenges that exist. It is also difficult for most people to understand how value-added estimates are generated because they are often derived from complex statistical models.

---

[1] In this report, for the sake of simplicity, "educational programs" refers to instructional programs as well as policy interventions, such as reducing class sizes.

In an effort to help policy makers understand the current strengths and limitations of value-added models, as well as to make decisions about whether to implement them in their jurisdictions, the National Research Council and the National Academy of Education jointly held a workshop on the topic on November 13 and 14, 2008, in Washington, DC. The workshop was funded by the Carnegie Corporation.

A committee chaired by Henry Braun of Boston College planned and facilitated the workshop. The event was designed to cover several topics related to value-added models: goals and uses, measurement issues, analytic issues, and possible consequences. The committee identified experts in each of these areas to write papers for presentation at the workshop and to serve as discussants. The workshop agenda and a list of participants appear in Appendix A. Biographical sketches of committee members and staff appear in Appendix B. The background papers and workshop transcript are posted on the National Research Council website at http://www7.nationalacademies.org/bota/VAM_Workshop_Agenda.html.

This report documents the information provided in the workshop presentations and discussions. Its purpose is to lay out the key ideas that emerged from the two-day workshop and should be viewed as an initial step in examining the research and applying it in specific policy circumstances. The statements in the report are confined to the material presented by the workshop speakers and participants. Neither the workshop nor this summary is intended as a comprehensive review of what is known about value-added methodology, although it is a general reflection of the literature. The presentations and discussions were limited by the time available for the workshop.

Although this report was prepared by the committee, it does not represent findings or recommendations that can be attributed to the committee members. The report summarizes views expressed by workshop participants, and the committee is responsible only for its overall quality and accuracy as a record of what transpired at a two-day event. The workshop was also not designed to generate consensus conclusions or recommendations but focused instead on the identification of ideas, themes, and considerations that contribute to understanding the current role of value-added models in educational settings.

GOALS OF VALUE-ADDED MODELING

The term "value-added" is used in manufacturing to refer to the difference between the value of the output and the cost of the raw materials. In education, the term is used more loosely because value-added in terms of changes in test scores is less tangible than value-added in terms of some real currency.[2] McCaffrey and Lockwood (2008) explain that while the origins of using value-added methods to estimate teacher effects date back over 30 years (Hanushek, 1972; Murnane, 1975), interest in these methods grew precipitously following the publication of a technical report by Sanders and Rivers in 1996. They found that teacher effects, estimated using student test score trajectories, predict student outcomes at least two years into the future. This finding suggested that teachers have persistent effects on their students' achievement and that the accumulation of these effects could be substantial. The following year, Sanders and his colleagues published another paper claiming that teachers are the most important source of variation in student achievement (Wright, Horn, and Sanders, 1997). Interest in value-added modeling was further stoked by other research findings indicating that the variability among teachers was large and that value-added estimates of teacher effects predict students' future test outcomes.

The number of jurisdictions that are using (or are interested in using) value-added models is increasing rapidly as many district, state, and federal education leaders look for new and better ways to measure school and teacher effectiveness. Tennessee has the best known value-added system; the results are used for school and teacher improvement. The Dallas school system also uses a value-added model for teacher evaluation. In 2008, Ohio began using a value-added model as one component of its state accountability system, to show how much schools and districts are adding to their students' learning over the course of one or more school years (Public Impact, 2008).

HOW VALUE-ADDED MODELS ARE DIFFERENT FROM OTHER EVALUATION MODELS

Several types of test-based evaluation models are currently used for education decision making. These include status models, cohort-to-cohort change models, growth models, and value-added models. Each type of model is designed to answer a different set of policy-relevant questions.

1. *Status models* give a snapshot of student performance[3] at a point in time, which is often compared with an established target. For example, the mean test score for a subgroup of students or a

---

[2]Another difference is that, in economics, value-added is defined absolutely, whereas in educational evaluation it is defined normatively, for example, relative to the gains made by other teachers. Nonetheless, the use of the term is well established in education and is used in this report.

[3]In this report, "performance" refers to demonstrated skill at a point in time (status), whereas "improvement" refers to change in performance over a period of time.

school can be compared with the state's annual target to determine if the school has met the state goal. A status model is useful if one wants to answer such questions as "What percentage of students in the state is performing at the proficient level this year?" "Has school X met the state proficiency target this year?"

2. *Cohort-to-cohort change models* can be used to measure the change in test results for a teacher, school, or state by comparing status at two points in time—but not for the same students. For example, the percentage proficient for this year's fourth graders in reading can be compared with that of last year's fourth graders. A cohort-to-cohort change model answers the question, "Are students at a certain grade level doing better this year in comparison to the students who were in the same grade last year?"

3. *Growth models* measure student achievement by tracking the test scores of the same students from one year to the next to determine the extent of their progress. Gain scores can be computed to compare the performance of the current year's fourth graders with that of the same group of students last year, when they were in third grade. This type of model is preferable if one wants to know "how much, on average, did students' performance change between grade X and grade Y?" There might also be a statewide growth target that subgroups or school systems must meet. Accountability systems built on growth models give teachers and schools credit if their students show improvement, regardless of whether they were high-performing or low-performing to begin with. However, growth models usually do not control for student or school background factors, and therefore they do not attempt to address which factors are responsible for student growth.

4. *Value-added models,* the focus of this report, are statistical models, often complex, that attempt to attribute some fraction of student achievement growth over time to certain schools, teachers, or programs. These models address such questions as "How did the contribution of school X (or teacher X) to student improvement compare with that of the average school (or teacher)?" Or equivalently, "How much of the change in student performance can be attributed to students attending one school (or one teacher's class) rather than another?" To isolate school, teacher, or program effects, at least two years of students' test scores are taken into account, sometimes along with other student and school-level variables, such as poverty, family background, or quality of school leadership. With some models, the value-added estimate for a school or a teacher is the difference between the observed improvement of the students and the expected improvement

(after taking account of differences among students that might be related to their academic achievement). For other models, as we shall see, the interpretation is not quite so straightforward; nonetheless, a value-added estimate is meant to approximate the contribution of the school, teacher, or program to student performance.[4]

In this report, we use the general term "evaluation system" to refer to any of the models (alone or in combination) described above, that are used to evaluate student achievement for the purposes of research, program evaluation, school or teacher improvement, or accountability. The design of an evaluation system and the decision as to whether a value-added model is appropriate will be shaped both by technical and political constraints, as well as by the resources available. It is important that the values (or goals) of education decision makers and their constituents be made explicit. In some instances, the schools, teachers, or programs identified as "best" based on a value-added analysis may not be regarded as "best" with respect to other criteria, because the value-added model gives greater weight to certain test score patterns than to others.

For example, if the designers of an accountability system are particularly concerned with all students reaching a certain level of proficiency, then a status model, such as that mandated by the No Child Left Behind legislation, might be an appropriate basis for determining rewards. However, the trade-off will be that some schools starting out with high-achieving students but having low value-added scores will be rewarded (or not sanctioned) by the system, while some schools starting out with low-achieving students but having high value-added scores will be identified as needing improvement (and sanctioned). The latter schools may be generally regarded as effective in helping their students make greater-than-average progress, although many will not have reached the proficient level. Thus, there would be a disjuncture between success-

---

[4]There is another category of models that is similar to value-added models but does not use students' prior test scores. Referred to as adjusted status models, they use statistical techniques to "adjust" average student achievement across units of analysis (i.e., schools, teachers, or programs) by accounting for differences in student composition or other factors. In effect, such models attempt to compare outcomes for similar units. If, for example, students whose parents have college degrees tend to have higher test scores than students whose parents have lower educational attainment, then the average student achievement (status) scores of schools with a higher percentage of college-educated parents will be adjusted downward while the average scores of schools with a lower percentage of college-educated parents will be adjusted upward. Such models are a first step toward true value-added models, but they do not make use of valuable information on students' prior performance.

ful schools using the value-added criterion and those that are accorded rewards.

If, however, the designers of the evaluation system are most concerned about identifying which teachers and schools are most effective, relative to other teachers and schools, in contributing to their students' growth in achievement over the course of the school year, then estimates of a value-added model might be a good basis for determining rewards. Note, however, that growth can be defined in many ways: it can be average gains along a conventional test score scale, the change in the fraction of students who meet or exceed a predetermined standard, or the difference between actual and expected average growth. The choice of the growth criterion is critical to achieving the desired impact, and each choice leads to different trade-offs.[5]

If the criterion is the average gain (or something akin to it), then the trade-off will be that teachers will not be held to the same absolute standard of achievement for all students. In other words, a teacher who raises her low performers' achievement more than other teachers with similar students will be considered more effective, but those students still may not be reaching the desired levels of achievement. If values and trade-offs are made explicit when the evaluation system is first conceived, then the system is more likely to be designed coherently, with a better chance of achieving the desired goals. In practice, policy makers' goals are usually more ambitious than statistical methodology and data quality can support.

THE PROBLEM THAT VALUE-ADDED METHODS AIM TO ADDRESS: NONRANDOM ASSIGNMENT OF STUDENTS

Currently, the most common way of reporting school test results is simply in terms of the percentage of students who score at the proficient level or above. However, it is widely recognized among education researchers and practitioners that school rankings based on unadjusted test scores are highly correlated with students' socioeconomic status (SES). Even students' rates of growth in achievement are statistically related to SES, with those who start out with higher scores typically gaining at faster rates (Willms, 2008). School achievement is cumulative in nature, in that it is the result of the input of past teachers, classroom peers, actions taken by

---

[5]Considerable effort has been devoted to elucidating the advantages and disadvantages of the different growth criteria that have been proposed. Note that designers may well have multiple goals, in which case they could construct different indices (each with its own "order of merit"). One or more of the indices could be related to a value-added analysis. Rewards or sanctions would then be based on some combination of the different indices.

administrators, and so on (Harris and Sass, 2005). Furthermore, students' current achievement is very much a function of out-of-school experiences, including inputs from families and communities. Under the most widely used evaluation models (status and cohort-to-cohort change), teachers and school administrators often argue that they are being unfairly judged since students' current test scores are greatly influenced by factors beyond their control and, moreover, that these factors are unevenly distributed across schools and between classrooms within a school.

Status models can be appropriate for making judgments about the achievement level of students at a particular school for a given year, whereas cohort-to-cohort models are better at tracking whether a school is improving, but both are less useful for comparing the effectiveness of teachers or instructional practices, either within or across schools. They do not disentangle the effects of status and progress. As Derek Briggs explained at the workshop, it could be that some schools or teachers whose students attain a high percentage proficient are actually making little progress. Such schools or teachers may be considered adequate simply because they happen to have the good fortune of enrolling students who were performing well to start with. There are also some schools or teachers who attain a low percentage proficient but whose students are making good progress, and such schools are not given credit under a status model. Likewise, cohort-to-cohort models do not take into account changes in the school population from year to year. Thus, changes in this criterion can be due to both actual changes in the school's effectiveness and differences in the student populations on relevant characteristics. The goal of value-added modeling is to make the sorts of distinctions illustrated in Figure 1-1.

It is interesting to note that, in past years, many states have presented

Achievement Level	II. High Achievement, Low Value-Added	I. High Achievement, High Value-Added
	III. Low Achievement, Low Value-Added	IV. Low Achievement, High Value-Added

Value-Added Modeling Estimates

FIGURE 1-1 Possible use of value-added results to classify schools in an accountability system.
SOURCE: Briggs (2008).

test results in *league tables*, which rank schools in order of average achievement. Schools are sometimes organized into strata that are determined by the SES profiles of their students. The intention is to remind the public that all schools are not directly comparable because they serve very different populations of students and to forestall complaints by schools that broad comparisons are unfair. At the workshop, Doug Willms referred to such stratified league tables as a sort of simplified version of statistical matching. Value-added models offer the promise of more sophisticated and rigorous approaches for leveling the playing field—that is, for taking into account students' background characteristics when comparing achievement across schools or teachers. But even here, there is need for caution; value-added modeling can make the playing field more level, but it can also reverse the tilt.[6]

A related way of thinking about value-added models is that they are "an attempt to capture the virtues of a randomized experiment when one has not been conducted" (Organisation for Economic Co-operation and Development, 2008, p. 108). Ideally, causal inferences are best drawn from randomized experiments that include large numbers of subjects, such as those typically conducted in agriculture or medicine. In the simplest version, there are two groups: an experimental group that receives the treatment and a control group that does not. Individuals are first randomly selected and then randomly assigned to one of the two groups. The difference in average outcomes for the two groups is a measure of the relative effectiveness of the treatment. To compare the effectiveness of two schools using an experimental design, students would need to be randomly assigned to the two schools, and achievement outcomes would be compared. However, in educational settings, random assignment is generally not feasible. As workshop presenter Dale Ballou noted, non-random assignment is pervasive in education, resulting from decisions by parents and school administrators: residential location decisions (often influenced by the perceived quality of local schools); parental requests for particular teachers or other efforts to influence teacher assignment; administrative decisions to place particular students with particular teachers—sometimes to improve the quality of the teacher-student match, sometimes as a form of favoritism shown to teachers or parents. Discussion leader Judith Singer summed up by saying that, with value-added methods, one is trying to develop "analytic fixes or measurement fixes, for

---

[6]"Reversing the tilt" means to carry out statistical adjustments that lead to increased bias in estimates of value-added. Building on the example in footnote 4, suppose that schools enrolling students with higher parental education are actually more effective than schools enrolling students with lower parental education. In this case adjusting for parental education could underestimate differences in effectiveness among schools.

what is basically a design problem: students are not randomly assigned to teachers [or schools]."

VALUE-ADDED MODELING AND THE
NO CHILD LEFT BEHIND ACT

Under NCLB, the key objective for a school or district is to make "adequate yearly progress." This requires meeting state-set targets for the percentage of students who score at or above the proficient level on the state's reading and mathematics tests. (The targets must increase over time to reach the ultimate goal of 100 percent proficiency in 2014.) This is a status model because it employs a snapshot of student performance at a certain point in time compared with a given target. The law's "safe harbor" provision provides an alternative, allowing schools to make adequate yearly progress even if they do not meet proficiency targets, under the condition that they reduce the percentage of students below the proficient level by at least 10 percent.

A number of problems with status models discussed at the workshop have already been mentioned. Another difficulty is that the percentage proficient, the focus of NCLB, gives an incomplete view of student achievement. It does not provide information about the progress of students who are above or below that level. By contrast, value-added models take into account test score trajectories at all achievement levels. Furthermore, the percentage proficient is a problematic way to measure achievement gaps among subgroups of students. The location of the proficiency cut score in relation to the score distributions of the subgroups makes a difference in the size of achievement gaps as measured by the percentage proficient. The problem is exacerbated when looking at trends in achievement gaps (Holland, 2002).

Since the 2006-2007 school year, under the Growth Model Pilot Program, some states have been allowed by the U.S. Department of Education to experiment with using certain types of growth models in the determination of adequate yearly progress. Sometimes referred to as growth-to-a-standard models, they track individual students' growth in test scores, but with important caveats that make such models consistent with the intent of NCLB. First, showing growth in test scores alone does not excuse states from the goal of 100 percent proficiency in 2014 or from having to meet intermediate targets along the way. Guidance issued by the U.S. Department of Education indicates that states must use growth targets that are still oriented toward meeting specific annual proficiency targets (hence "growth to a standard"), rather than measures that determine whether schools or individual students meet or exceed "projected" or "expected" growth targets, as these "denote an empirically derived student performance score not necessarily related to the NCLB policy goals of universal proficiency" (U.S. Department of Education, 2009, p. 12). Second, making any adjustments for student background characteristics, such as race or income, in determining growth targets is not allowed; the concern is that lower targets may be assigned to specific groups of students. Not adjusting for student background is seen by some as one way of implementing a policy of high expectations for all, in contrast to most value-added models, which do control for background factors. For these reasons, value-added modeling cannot be used as a chief means to determine adequate yearly progress under NCLB, unless the model somehow incorporates these limitations. However, many participants argued that adjusting for background factors is a more appropriate approach to developing indicators of school effectiveness.

Workshop participant Adam Gamoran suggested that using imperfect value-added models would be better than retaining NCLB in its current form. He viewed value-added indicators as more informative than simple status comparisons and worried about the coming "train wreck" that might occur as more and more schools fail to meet the goal of 100 percent proficiency in 2014. However, other participants—Derek Briggs, Robert Gordon, John Easton, and others—favored using some combination of status and value-added (or simpler growth) indicators for accountability, perhaps with other metrics of school performance, rather than abandoning status indicators altogether. They argued for multiple measures that provide different perspectives on student achievement; status indicators provide information with respect to students' locations on the achievement continuum and have the advantage of being easy to understand.[7]

KEY CONCERNS

During the workshop, most of the participants expressed support for trying value-added models for various evaluation purposes but urged caution in using the results as the sole basis for making important decisions. Individuals' concerns ranged over a number of areas for which further development and analysis are needed. Some focused, for example, on problems with the tests that provide the raw data for value-added analyses; others were concerned with technical aspects of different value-added approaches, especially with sources of bias and imprecision; and still others focused on issues of transparency and public understanding of the results. Some of the concerns, such as the fact that tests are incomplete measures of student achievement, are general problems that arise

---

[7]As noted in later chapters, a status indicator places fewer demands on the assessment system.

with all types of test-based evaluation models (including value-added ones), whereas others, such as the need for interval scales, are specific to particular classes of value-added models.[8]

Box 1-1 summarizes areas of concern that were discussed at the workshop, which are explained more fully in subsequent chapters of this report. The final chapter summarizes a number of questions that policy makers should consider if they are thinking about using value-added indicators for decision making.

---

[8]Approaches to value-added models that employ linear models implicitly treat the score scale as having interval scale properties.

BOX 1-1
Participants' Concerns About Implementation of Value-Added Models

The workshop presentations and discussions raised a number of concerns about value-added methodology, which are dealt with at greater length in the chapters of the report.

Uses and Possible Consequences (Chapters 1 and 2)

- *Values and trade-offs.* Although value-added models offer insights that other indicators do not provide, they do not serve all policy purposes. In deciding whether they should be included in an evaluation system, designers need to be clear from the start about their values and objectives, and to understand the trade-offs among them.
- *High-stakes versus low-stakes uses.* When value-added estimates are used to make high-stakes decisions about individual people or institutions—such as about teacher pay or whether a school should face sanctions—the value-added models must be held to higher standards of reliability and validity than when the stakes are low (e.g., providing information to guide professional development choices of teachers). In the view of many at the workshop, evidence for the reliability and validity of value-added estimates is not sufficiently strong to support their use as the sole basis for high-stakes decisions, and therefore they are most appropriately used in combination with other indicators for such purposes.
- *Incentives and consequences.* If value-added indicators are part of an accountability system, they are likely to change educators' behavior and to lead to unintended consequences, as well as intended ones. It is important for system designers to consider the incentives that value-added indicators may create for teachers, administrators, and even students.
- *Attribution.* In situations in which there is team teaching or a coordinated emphasis within a school (e.g., writing across the curriculum), is it appropriate to attribute students' learning to a single teacher?

Measurement Issues (Chapter 3)

- *Tests are incomplete measures of student achievement.* Value-added estimates are based on test scores that reflect a narrower set of educational goals than most parents and educators have for students. If this narrowing is severe, and if the test does not cover the most important state content standards in sufficient breadth or depth, then the value-added results will offer limited or even misleading information about the effectiveness of schools, teachers, or programs.
- *Measurement error.* Test scores are not perfectly precise. Despite all the efforts that test developers devote to creating tests that accurately measure a student's knowledge and skills, all test scores are susceptible to measurement error at the individual and aggregate levels, and this measurement error contributes to uncertainty in value-added estimates.

- *Interval scale.* To provide a consistent ranking of schools', teachers', or programs' value-added, one important assumption underlying value-added analyses employing regression models is that the tests used in the analyses are reported on an equal interval scale. This means that a 10-point increase from 30 to 40 should be equivalent a 10-point gain from 60 to 70 (or any other region of the scale) and should be valued equally. Most (if not all) tests do not meet this requirement, at least not exactly. The degree of departure from the assumption bears on the validity of value-added interpretations.
- *Vertical linking of tests.* Some value-added models require vertically linked test score scales; that is, the scores on tests from different grades are linked to a common scale so that students' scores from different grades can be compared directly. In other cases, raw test scores from different grades are placed on a common scale by the test vendor before they are reported to the state. A number of researchers have focused on choices in test design and/or linking strategies and how they affect the properties of the vertical scales and, ultimately, the value-added estimates that are produced.
- *Models of learning.* Some researchers argue that value-added models would be more useful if there were better content standards that laid out developmental pathways of learning and highlighted critical transitions; tests could then be aligned to such developmental standards. This sort of coherence across grade levels could improve both the statistical characteristics and interpretability of value-added estimates.

Analytic Issues (Chapter 4)

- *Bias.* In order to tackle the problem of nonrandom assignment of students to teachers and teachers to schools, value-added modeling adjusts for preexisting differences among students, using prior test scores and sometimes other student and school characteristics. The models can consistently overestimate or underestimate school or program effects, depending on the type of model, as well as the number and statistical characteristics of the predictor variables that are included.
- *Precision and stability.* Research on the precision of value-added estimates consistently finds large sampling errors. Small sample sizes are a particular problem when estimating teacher effects, because teachers often have only a relatively small number of students in a given year. If the number of students per teacher is small, just a few poorly performing students can substantially lower the estimate of a teacher's effectiveness, and just a few very high performing students can substantially raise it. Small sample sizes can result in estimated teacher or school effects that fluctuate substantially from year to year for reasons unrelated to their actual performance. Other causes of instability are real differences in a teacher's performance from year to year and sources of variation due to changes in the teaching context across years (e.g., school leadership, peer effects, and student mobility).

continued

BOX 1-1   Continued

- *Data quality.* Missing or faulty data can have a negative impact on the precision and stability of value-added estimates and can also contribute to bias. While data quality is important for any evaluation system, the requirements for value-added models tend to be greater because longitudinal data are needed, often for a variety of variables.
- *Complexity versus transparency.* More complex value-added models tend to have better technical qualities. However, there is always the point at which adding more complexity to the model results in little or no additional practical advantage while, at the same time, making it more difficult for educators and the public to understand. A challenge is to find the right balance between complexity and transparency.

2

Uses and Consequences of Value-Added Models

This chapter provides an overview of how value-added models are currently being used for research, school and teacher improvement, program evaluation, and school and teacher accountability. These purposes can overlap to some extent, and often an evaluation system will be used for more than one purpose. The use of these models for educational purposes is growing fast. For example, the Teacher Incentive Fund program of the U.S. Department of Education, created in 2006, has distributed funds to over 30 jurisdictions to experiment with alternate compensation systems for teachers and principals—particularly systems that reward educators (at least in part) for increases in student achievement as measured by state tests.[1] Some districts, such as the Dallas Independent School District (Texas), Guilford County Schools (North Carolina), and Memphis City Schools (Tennessee) are using value-added models to evaluate teacher performance (Center for Educator Compensation Reform, no date; Isenberg, 2008).

If the use of value-added modeling becomes widespread, what are the likely consequences? These models, particularly when used in a high-stakes accountability setting, may create strong incentives for teachers and administrators to change their behavior. The avowed intention is for educators to respond by working harder or by incorporating different teaching strategies to improve student achievement. However, perverse incentives may also be

---

[1]The amount of the bonus linked to student achievement is small; much of the money goes to professional development. Additional funds for the Teacher Incentive Fund are supposed to come from the American Recovery and Reinvestment Act.

created, resulting in unintended negative consequences. On one hand, for example, since a value-added system compares the performance of teachers relative to one another, it could reduce teacher cooperation within schools, depending on how the incentives are structured. On the other hand, if school-level value-added is rewarded, it can create a "free rider" problem whereby some shirkers benefit from the good work of their colleagues, without putting forth more effort themselves. Because the implementation of value-added models in education has so far been limited, there is not much evidence about their consequences. At the workshop, some clues as to how educators might respond were provided by the case of a program instituted in New York that used an adjusted status model to monitor the effectiveness of heart surgeons in the state's hospitals. We provide below some examples of how value-added models have recently been used in education for various purposes.

SOME RECENT USES

Research

Value-added models can be useful for conducting exploratory research on educational interventions because they aim to identify the contributions of certain programs, teachers, or schools when a true experimental design is not feasible.

Workshop presenter John Easton has been studying school reform in Chicago for about 20 years. He and his colleagues used surveys of educators to identify essential supports for school success (inclusive leadership, parents' community ties, professional capacity, student-centered learning climate, and ambitious instruction). The team then used a value-added analysis to provide empirical evidence that these fundamentals were indeed strongly associated with school effectiveness. As a result of this research, the Chicago Public School system has adopted these essential supports as its "five fundamentals for school success" (Easton, 2008).

Value-added models have also been used by researchers to gauge the relationship of various teacher qualifications (such as licensure, certification, years of experience, advanced degrees) to student progress. Workshop discussant Helen Ladd described her research, which applied a value-added model to data from North Carolina to explore the relationship between teacher credentials and students' performance on end-of-course exams at the high school level (Clotfelter, Ladd, and Vigdor, 2007). The researchers found that teacher credentials are positively correlated with student achievement. One problem Ladd's studies identified is that teachers with weaker credentials were concentrated in higher poverty schools, and the apparent effects of having low-credentialed teachers in high school was great, particularly for African American students: "We conclude that if the teachers assigned to black students had the same credentials on average as those assigned to white students, the achievement difference between black and white students would be reduced by about one third" (Clotfelter, Ladd, and Vigdor, 2007, p. 38).

Easton argued that more research studies are needed using value-added models, as an essential first step in exploring their possible uses for accountability or other high-stakes purposes. "The more widely circulated research using value-added metrics as outcomes there is, the more understanding there will be about [how] they can be used most successfully and what their limits are" (Easton, 2008, p. 9).

School or Teacher Improvement

Value-added models are intended to help identify schools or teachers as more effective or less effective, as well as the areas in which they are differentially effective. Ideally, that can lead to further investigation and, ultimately, the adoption of improved instructional strategies. Value-added results might be used by teachers for self-improvement or target setting. At the school level, they might be used along with other measures to help identify the subjects, grades, and groups of students for which the school is adding most value and where improvement is needed. Value-added analyses of the relationships between school inputs and school performance could suggest which strategies are most productive, leading to ongoing policy adjustments and reallocation of resources. The models might also be used to create projections of school performance that can assist in planning, resource allocation, and decision making. In these ways, value-added results could be used by teachers and schools as an early warning signal.

Perhaps the best-known value-added model used for teacher evaluation and improvement is the Education Value Added Assessment System (EVAAS), which has been used in Tennessee since 1993. "The primary purpose . . . is to provide information about how effective a school, system, or teacher has been in leading students to achieve normal academic gain over a three year period." (Sanders and Horn, 1998, p. 250). The system was created by William Sanders and his colleagues, and this model (or variations) have been tried in a number of different school districts. EVAAS-derived reports on teacher effectiveness are made available to teachers and administrators but are not made public. State legislation requires that EVAAS results are to be part of the evaluation of those teachers for whom such data are available (those who teach courses tested by the statewide assessment program). How large a role the estimates of effectiveness are to play in teacher evaluation is left up to the district, although EVAAS reports cannot be the sole source of information in a teacher's evaluation. They are used to create individualized professional development plans for teachers, and subsequent EVAAS reports can be used to judge the extent to which improved teacher performance has resulted from these plans (Sanders and Horn, 1998).

Program Evaluation

When used for program evaluation, value-added models can provide information about which types of local or national school programs or policy initiatives are adding the most value and which are not, in terms of student achievement. These might include initiatives as diverse as a new curriculum, decreased class size, and approaches to teacher certification.

The Teach For America (TFA) Program recruits graduates of four-year colleges and universities to teach in public schools (K-12) in high-poverty districts. It receives funding from both private sources and the federal government. In recent years, the program has placed between 2,000 and 4,000 teachers annually. Recruits agree to teach for two years at pay comparable to that of other newly hired teachers. After an intensive summer-long training session, they are placed in the classroom, with mentoring and evaluation provided throughout the year. The program has been criticized because many believe that this alternate route to teaching is associated with lower quality teaching. There is also the concern that, because the majority of participants leave their positions upon completing their two-year commitment, students in participating districts are being taught by less experienced (and therefore less effective) teachers. Xu, Hannaway, and Taylor (2007) used an adjusted status model (similar to a value-added model but does not use prior test scores) to investigate these criticisms. Using data on secondary school students and teachers from North Carolina,[2] the researchers found that TFA teachers were more effective in raising exam scores than other teachers, even those with more experience: "TFA teachers are more effective than the teachers who would otherwise be in the classroom in their stead" (p. 23). This finding may be dependent on the poor quality of the experienced teachers in the types of high-poverty urban districts served by the program.

---

[2]It is important to note that the researchers used a "cross-subject fixed-effects model" that employed student performance across a variety of subjects rather than student performance on tests taken in past years. This strategy was required because it was a study of secondary school performance, and prior scores in courses such as biology were not available.

School or Teacher Accountability

In an accountability context, consequences are attached to value-added results in order to provide incentives to teachers and school administrators to improve student performance. They might be used for such decisions as whether the students in a school are making appropriate progress for the school to avoid sanctions or receive rewards, or whether a teacher should get a salary increase. School accountability systems that use value-added models would provide this information to the public—taxpayers might be informed as to whether tax money is being used efficiently, and users might be able to choose schools on a more informed basis. At this time, many policy makers are seriously considering using value-added results for accountability, and there is much discussion about these possible uses. But the design of a model might differ depending on whether the goal is to create incentives to improve the performance of certain students, to weed out weak teachers, or to inform parents about the most effective schools for their children.

In August 2008, Ohio began implementing a program that incorporates a value-added model. The program chosen by the state is based on the EVAAS model William Sanders developed for Tennessee. Ohio's accountability system employs multiple measures, whereby schools are assigned ratings on the basis of a set of indicators. Until recently, the measures were (1) the percentage of students reaching the proficient level on state tests, as well as graduation and attendance rates; (2) whether the school made adequate yearly progress under No Child Left Behind; (3) a performance index that combines state tests results; and (4) a measure of improvement in the performance index. Ohio replaced the last component with a value-added indicator. Instead of simply comparing a student's gain with the average gain, the model develops a customized prediction of each student's progress on the basis of his or her own academic record, as well as that of other students over multiple years, with statewide test performance serving as an anchor. So the value-added gain is the difference between a student's score in a given subject and the score predicted by the model. The school-level indicator is based on the averages of the value-added gains of its students. Consequently, Ohio will now be rating schools using estimated value-added as one component among others. The model will be used only at the school level, not the teacher level, and only at the elementary and middle grades. Because tests are given only once in high school, in tenth grade, growth in student test scores cannot be determined directly (Public Impact, 2008).

There are examples of using value-added modeling to determine teacher performance pay at the district level. The national Teacher Advancement Program (TAP) is a merit pay program for teachers that uses a value-added model of student test score growth as a factor in determining teacher pay. About 6,000 teachers in 50 school districts nationwide participate in this program, which was established by the Milken Family Foundation in 1999. Participating districts essentially create an alternate pay and training system for teachers, based on multiple career paths, ongoing professional development, accountability for student performance, and performance pay. TAP uses a value-added model to determine contributions to student achievement gains at both the classroom and school levels. Teachers are awarded bonuses based on their scores in a weighted performance evaluation that measures mastery of effective classroom practices (50 percent), student achievement gains for their classrooms (30 percent), and school-wide achievement gains (20 percent) (http://www.talentedteachers.org/index.taf).

It should be noted that a number of other states have had performance pay programs for teachers, including Alaska, Arizona, Florida,[3] and Minnesota, where growth in test scores is a factor, usually a rather small one, in determining teacher pay. However, these systems are based on growth models, not value-added models. Unlike value-added models, the growth models used do not control for background factors, other than students' achievement in the previous year.

Low Stakes Versus High Stakes

A frequent theme throughout the workshop was that when test-based indicators are used to make important decisions, especially ones that affect individual teachers, administrators, or students, the results must be held to higher standards of reliability and validity than when the stakes are lower. However, drawing the line between high and low stakes is not always straightforward. As Henry Braun noted, what is "high stakes for somebody may be low stakes for someone else." For example, simply reporting school test results through the media or sharing teacher-level results among staff—even in the absence of more concrete rewards or sanctions—can be experienced as high stakes for some schools or teachers. Furthermore, in a particular evaluation, stakes are often different for various stakeholders, such as students, teachers, and principals.

Participants generally referred to exploratory research as a low-stakes use and school or teacher accountability as a high-stakes uses. Using value-added results for school or teacher improvement, or program evaluation, fell somewhere in between, depending on the particular circum-

---

[3] Interestingly, the Florida merit pay program proved very unpopular after it was discovered that teachers in the most affluent schools were the ones benefiting the most. Most of the participating districts turned down the additional money after its first year of implementation.

stances. For example, as Derek Briggs pointed out, using a value-added model for program evaluation could be high stakes if the studies were part of the What Works Clearinghouse, sponsored by the U.S. Department of Education.

In any case, it is important for designers of an evaluation system to first set out the standards for the properties they desire of the evaluation model and then ask if value-added approaches satisfy them. For example, if one wants transparency to enable personnel actions to be fully defensible, a very complex value-added model may well fail to meet the requirement. If one wants all schools in a state to be assessed using the same tests and with adjustments for background factors, value-added approaches do meet the requirement.

POSSIBLE INCENTIVES AND CONSEQUENCES

To date, there is little relevant research in education on the incentives created by value-added evaluation systems and the effects on school culture, teacher practice, and student outcomes. The workshop therefore addressed the issue of the possible consequences of using value-added models for high-stakes purposes by looking at high-quality studies about their use in other contexts. Ashish Jha presented a paper on the use of an adjusted status model (see footnote 4, Chapter 1) in New York State for the purpose of improving health care. The Cardiac Surgery Reporting System (CSRS) was introduced in 1990 to monitor the performance of surgeons performing coronary bypass surgeries. The New York Department of Health began to publicly report the performance of both hospitals and individual surgeons. Assessment of the performance of about 31 hospitals and 100 surgeons, as measured by risk-adjusted mortality rates, was freely available to New York citizens. In this application, the statistical model adjusted for patient risk, in a manner similar to the way models in education adjust for student characteristics. The model tried to address the question: How successful was the treatment by a certain doctor or hospital, given the severity of a patient's symptoms? The risk-adjustment model drew on the patients' clinical data (adequacy of heart function prior to surgery, condition of the kidneys, other factors associated with recovery, etc.).

In 1989, prior to the introduction of CSRS, the risk-adjusted in-hospital mortality rate for patients undergoing heart surgery was 4.2 percent; eight years after the introduction of CSRS, this rate was cut in half to 2.1 percent, the lowest in the nation. Empirical evaluations of CSRS, as well as anecdotal evidence, indicate that a number of surgeons with high adjusted mortality rates stopped practicing in New York after public reporting began. Poor-performing surgeons were four times more likely to stop practicing in New York within two years of the release of a negative report. (However, many simply moved to neighboring states.) Several of the hospitals with the worst mortality rates revamped their cardiac surgery programs. This was precisely what was hoped for by the state and, from this point of view, the CSRS program was a success.

However, there were reports of unintended consequences of this intervention. Some studies indicated that surgeons were less likely to operate on sicker patients, although others contradicted this claim. There was also some evidence that documentation of patients' previous conditions changed in such a way as to make them appear sicker, thereby reducing a provider's risk-adjusted mortality rate. Finally, one study conducted by Jha and colleagues (2008) found that the introduction of CSRS had a significant deleterious effect on access to surgery for African American patients. The proportion of African American patients dropped, presumably because surgeons perceived them as high risk and therefore were less willing to perform surgery on them. It took almost a decade before the racial composition of patients reverted to pre-CSRS proportions.

This health care example illustrates that, if value-added models are to be used in an education accountability context, with the intention of changing the behavior of teachers and administrators, one can expect both intended and unintended consequences. The adjustment process should be clearly explained, and an incentive structure should be put into place that minimizes perverse incentives. Discussant Helen Ladd emphasized transparency: "Teachers need to understand what goes into the outcome measures, what they can do to change the outcome, and to have confidence that the measure is consistently and fairly calculated. . . . The system is likely to be most effective if teachers believe the measure treats them fairly in the sense of holding them accountable for things that are under their control."

Workshop participants noted a few ways that test-based accountability systems have had unintended consequences in the education context. For example, Ladd (2008) gave the example of South Carolina, which experimented in the 1980s with a growth model (not a value-added model). It was hoped that the growth model would be more appropriate and useful than the status model that had been used previously. The status model was regarded as faulty because the results largely reflected socioeconomic status (SES). It was found, however, that the growth model results still favored schools serving more advantaged students, which were then more likely to be eligible for rewards than schools serving low-income students and minority students. State and school officials were concerned. In response, they created a school classification system based mainly on the average SES of the students in the schools. Schools were then compared only with other schools in the same category, with rewards equitably distributed across categories. This was widely regarded as fair. However, one result was that schools at the boundaries had an incentive to try to get into a lower SES classification in order to increase their chances of receiving a reward.

Sean Reardon pointed out a similar situation based on the use of a value-added model in San Diego (Koedel and Betts, 2009). Test scores from fourth grade students (along with their matched test scores from third and second grade) indicated that teachers were showing the greatest gains among low-performing students. Possible explanations were that the best teachers were concentrated in the classes with students with the lowest initial skills (which was unlikely), or that there was a ceiling effect or some other consequence of test scaling, such that low-performing students were able to show much greater gains than higher-performing students. It was difficult to determine the exact cause, but had the model been implemented for teacher pay or accountability purposes, the teachers would have had an incentive to move to those schools serving students with low SES, where they could achieve the greatest score gains. Reardon observed, "That could be a good thing. If I think I am a really good teacher with this population of students, then the league [tables] make me want to move to a school where I teach that population of students, so that I rank relatively high in that league." The disadvantage of using indicators based on students' status is that one can no longer reasonably compare the effectiveness of a teacher who teaches low-skilled students with that of a teacher who teaches high-skilled students or compare schools with very different populations.

Adam Gamoran suggested that the jury has not reached a verdict on whether a performance-based incentive system that was intended to motivate teachers to improve would be better than the current system, which rewards teachers on the basis of experience and professional qualifications. However, he noted that the current system also has problematic incentives: it provides incentives for all teachers, regardless of their effectiveness, to stay in teaching, because the longer they stay, the more their salary increases. After several years of teaching, teachers reach the point at which there are huge benefits for persisting and substantial costs to leaving.

An alternative is a system that rewards more effective teachers and encourages less effective ones to leave. A value-added model that evaluates teachers has the potential to become part of such a system. At the moment, such a system is problematic, in part because of the imprecision of value-added teacher estimates. Gamoran speculated that a pay-for-performance system for teachers based on current value-added models would probably result in short-term improvement for staying, because teachers would work harder for a bonus. He judged that the long-term effects are less clear, however, due to the imprecision of the models under some conditions.

Given this imprecision, a teacher's bonus might be largely a matter of luck rather than a matter of doing something better. "Teachers will figure that out pretty quickly. The system will lose its incentive power. Why bother to try hard? Why bother to seek out new strategies? Just trust to luck to get the bonus one year if not another." These potential problems might be reduced by combining a teacher's results across several (e.g., three) years, thus improving the precision of teachers' value-added estimates.

Several workshop participants made the point that, even without strong, tangible rewards or sanctions for teachers or administrators, an accountability system will still induce incentives. Ben Jensen commented that when value-added scores are made publicly available, they create both career and prestige incentives: "If I am a school principal, particularly at a school serving a poor community, [and] I have a high value-added score, I am going to put that on my CV and therefore, there is a real incentive effect." Brian Stecher also noted that for school principals in Dallas, which has a performance pay system, it is not always necessary to give a principal a monetary reward to change his or her behavior. There is the effect of competition: if a principal saw other principals receiving rewards and he or she did not get one, that tended to be enough to change behavior. The incentives created a dramatic shift in internal norms and cultures in the workplace and achieved the desired result.

NOT FOR ALL POLICY PURPOSES

Value-added models are not necessarily the best choice for all policy purposes; indeed, no single evaluation model is. For example, there is concern that adjusting for students' family characteristics and school contextual variables might reinforce existing disadvantages in schools with a high proportion of students with lower SES, by effectively setting lower expectations for those students. Another issue is that value-added results are usually normative: Schools or teachers are characterized as performing either above or below average compared with other units in the analysis, such as teachers in the same school, district, or perhaps state. In other words, estimates of value-added have meaning only in comparison to average estimated effectiveness. This is different from current systems of state accountability that are criterion-referenced, in which performance is described in relation to a standard set by the state (such as the proficient level). Dan McCaffrey explained that if the policy goal is for all students to reach a certain acceptable level of achievement, then it may not be appropriate to reward schools that are adding great value but still are not making enough progress.[4] From the perspective of students and their families, school value-added measures might be important, but they may also want to know the extent to which schools and students have met state standards.

CONCLUSION

Value-added models clearly have many potential uses in education. At the workshop, there was little concern about using them for exploratory research or to identify teachers who might benefit most from professional development. In fact, one participant argued that these types of low-stakes uses were needed to increase understanding about the strengths and limitations of different value-added approaches and to set the stage for their possible use for higher stakes purposes in the future.

There was a great deal of concern expressed, however, about using these models alone for high-stakes decisions—such as whether a school is in need of improvement or whether a teacher deserves a bonus, tenure, or promotion—given the current state of knowledge about the accuracy of value-added estimates. Most participants acknowledged that they would be uncomfortable basing almost any high-stakes decision on a single measure or indicator, such as a status determination. The rationales for participants' concerns are explained in the next two chapters.

---

[4]Of course, there can be disagreement as to whether this is a reasonable or appropriate goal.

3

Measurement Issues

Student test scores are at the heart of value-added analyses. All value-added models (VAMs) use patterns in test performance over time as the measure of student learning. Therefore, it is important to ensure that the test scores themselves can support the inferences made about the results from value-added analyses.

To date, most value-added research in education has been conducted by specialists in education statistics, as well as by economists who work in the area of education policy analysis. At the workshop, Dale Ballou, an economist, pointed out that "the question of what achievement tests measure and how they measure it is probably the [issue] most neglected by economists. . . . If tests do not cover enough of what teachers actually teach (a common complaint), the most sophisticated statistical analysis in the world still will not yield good estimates of value-added unless it is appropriate to attach zero weight to learning that is not covered by the test." As Mark Reckase, an educational testing expert noted, even the educational measurement literature on value-added models "makes little mention of the measurement requirements for using the models. For example, a summary of value-added research published by the American Educational Research Association (Zurawsky, 2004) only indicates that the tests need to be aligned to the state curriculum for them to be used for VAMs" (Reckase, 2008, p. 5).

Reckase further observed that, in the measurement literature, value-added methods have not made it to the point of being a "hot topic," and most people in the measurement community do not know what they are. Several workshop participants suggested that, given the push from policy makers to start using these models for educational improvement and accountability, the measurement field needs to step up to the challenge and make it a priority to address the issues in test design that would enhance the credibility of value-added analysis. More collaborative, cross-disciplinary work between VAM researchers from the disciplines of economics, statistics, and educational measurement will also be needed to resolve some of the difficult technical challenges.

The papers on value-added measurement issues that were prepared for the workshop consistently raised issues related to what tests measure, error associated with test scores, complexities of measuring growth, and the score scales that are used to report the results from tests. This chapter explains those issues and draws heavily from the workshop papers by Dale Ballou, Michael Kane, Michael Kolen, Robert Linn, Mark Reckase, and Doug Willms. More details can be found in those papers as well as in the workshop transcripts, which are posted at http://www7. nationalacademies.org/bota/VAM_Workshop_Agenda.html.

THE CONCEPT OF VALUE AND THE
MEASUREMENT OF VALUE-ADDED

To calculate value-added requires measurement of the value of both outputs and inputs. Imagine two factories that produce cars and trucks using only petroleum products (plastic, rubber) and steel as inputs. One factory produces 2,000 cars and 500 trucks per day, and the other produces 1,000 of each. Which produces more valuable outputs? The economists' answer is to measure value by the price of the goods. If trucks sell for twice as much as cars, the value of the output produced by the two factories is identical. If trucks are relatively more expensive, the second factory will produce output of greater value, and if they are relatively less expensive, it will produce output of lower value. Of course, this shows only the relative value of the outputs. One also needs to calculate the relative value of the inputs and the value of the outputs relative to the inputs. The existence of a price system solves that problem. But it is important to recognize that even here, the concept of value-added is narrow. If one does not believe that prices fully capture the social value of extracting the raw materials converting them to output, then the value-added measured by economists will not capture the social value-added of the factories.[1]

In some cases one can rank the productivity of the plants without

---

[1]There is an analogous situation in education, as many argue that test scores do not capture other important aspects of student development and, as a consequence, value-added estimates do not reflect schools' and teachers' contributions to that development.

a price system. If the two factories use the same raw materials, but one produces more cars and more trucks, then that factory has greater value-added (provided that both cars and trucks are good) regardless of the relative merit of cars and trucks. Similarly, if they produce the same output, but one uses less of each input, then it produces greater value-added.

In education, the calculation of value-added requires similar considerations of the value placed on different outcomes. Is producing two students with scores of 275 on the state test better or worse than producing one with a 250 and another with 300? And is it better or worse to take a student who scored 100 on last year's test to scoring 150 this year than to take a student from 200 to 300?

Any calculation of value-added is based only on those outputs and inputs that are measured. If the factories described above also produce pollution that is not measured, the economic value-added to society will be overestimated. In the same way, failing to measure important educational inputs or outputs because these are not easily captured by written tests will bias the measure of value-added in education.

It is not yet clear how important these concerns are in practice when using value-added modeling. If two schools have similar students initially, but one produces students with better test scores, it will have a higher measured value-added regardless of the scale chosen. Similarly, if they produce the same test scores, but one began with weaker students, the ranking of the schools will not depend on the scale. There are also issues of the weight the test accords to different content standards and the levels of difficulty of different questions. These and other measurement challenges that arise when using value-added methods are explained more fully in the sections that follow.

MEASUREMENT CHALLENGES

Tests Are Incomplete Measures of Achievement

It is not widely appreciated that all test results are estimates of student achievement that are incomplete in several respects (National Research Council, in press). This is an important issue that applies to all test-based evaluation models. A test covers only a small sample of knowledge and skills from the much larger subject domain that it is intended to represent (e.g., fourth grade reading, eighth grade mathematics), and the test questions are typically limited to a few formats (e.g., multiple choice or short answer). The measured domains themselves represent only a subset of the important goals of education; a state may test mathematics, reading, and science but not other domains that are taught, such as social studies, music, and computer skills. Furthermore, large-scale tests generally do not measure other important qualities that schools seek to foster in students but are more difficult to measure, such as intellectual curiosity, motivation, persistence in tackling difficult tasks, or the ability to collaborate well with others.

For these reasons, value-added estimates are based on a set of test scores that reflect a narrower set of educational goals than most parents and educators have for their students. If this narrowing is severe, and if the test does not cover the most important educational goals from state content standards in sufficient breadth or depth, then the value-added results will offer limited or even misleading information about the effectiveness of schools, teachers, or programs. For example, if a state's science standards emphasize scientific inquiry as an important goal, but the state test primarily assesses recall of science facts, then the test results are not an appropriate basis for using value-added models to estimate the effectiveness of science teachers with respect to the most valued educational goals. A science teacher who focuses instruction on memorization of facts may achieve a high value-added (thus appearing to be very effective), whereas one who emphasizes scientific inquiry may obtain a low value-added (thus appearing to be ineffective).

Robert Linn and other workshop participants raised the related issue of instructional sensitivity. In the testing literature, Popham (2007) explains that "an instructionally *sensitive* test would be capable of distinguishing between strong and weak instruction by allowing us to validly conclude that a set of students' high test scores are meaningfully, but not exclusively, attributable to effective instruction. . . . In contrast, an instructionally insensitive test would not allow us to distinguish accurately between strong and weak instruction" (pp. 146-147). This is relevant to value-added modeling because the models are meant to capture the component of learning attributable to the effort of the school, teacher, or program, separate from other factors. If the tests are not designed to fully capture the learning that is going on (or meant to go on) in the classroom, then educators cannot get "credit" for their work. For example, suppose that according to the state science standards, fourth grade science is more about facts, and inquiry is introduced in fifth grade, but both tests focus on facts. Then student learning with respect to inquiry will not be directly reflected in test performance, and the fifth grade teachers will not get adequate credit for their work. In such a case, it does not matter what other student or context factors are taken into account in the model, as the critical information about achievement is not there to begin with.

Lockwood and colleagues (2007) conducted research showing the impact of the choice of tests on teacher value-added estimates. They compared the results of value-added results for a large school district using two different subtests of the Stanford mathematics assessment for grades

6, 7, and 8: the procedures subtest and the problem-solving subtest. They used a wide range of models, ranging from simple gain score models to those using a variety of control variables. The estimated teacher effects for the two different subtests had generally low correlations regardless of which model was used to calculate the estimated effects. Their results demonstrate that "caution is needed when interpreting estimated teacher effects because there is the potential for teacher performance to depend on the skills that are measured by the achievement tests" (Lockwood et al., 2007, p. 56).

Measurement Error

Despite all the efforts that test developers devote to creating tests that accurately measure a student's knowledge and skills, all test scores are susceptible to measurement error. Measurement error results from the fact that the test items are a sample from a universe of relevant test items, which are administered to students at one time out of many possible times. An individual might perform slightly better or worse if a different set of questions had been chosen or the test had been given on a different day. For example, on a particular day there might be a disruption in the testing room, or a student may not physically feel well. Measurement error is also associated with item format. For multiple-choice items, student guessing is a source of error. For constructed-response items (short-answer or essay questions) that are scored by people rather than machines, there can be variation in the behavior of the people hired to score these questions.[2]

A student's test score can thus be thought of as a composite of his or her true skill level in the tested area as well as the random factors that can affect his or her performance, as well as the evaluation of that performance. *Reliability* is a measure of the extent to which these random factors contribute to students' observed scores. Another way of thinking of reliability is as a measure of the replicability of students' scores—if the same set of students took a parallel test on another day, how similar would their rankings be? Since inferences about teacher, school, or program effects are based on student test scores, test score reliability is an important consideration in value-added modeling.

Some models measure learning with gain scores (or change scores). Gain scores are computed by subtracting, for each student, the previous year's test score from the current year's test score. A benefit of using gain

---

[2]Individual scorers will differ from one another on both average stringency and variability. Scoring patterns of a particular individual will vary by time of day and over days. All these differences contribute to measurement error.

scores in value-added modeling is that students can serve as their own controls for prior achievement. One potential problem with gain scores, however, relates to measurement error. When a gain score is computed by subtracting the score at time 1 from the score at time 2, the difference in scores includes the measurement error from both testing occasions. The variability of the measurement error of the gain score will tend to be larger than the variability of the measurement error of either of its components. Thus, gain scores can be less reliable than either of the scores that were used to compute them. However, some researchers have argued that this simple logic does not necessarily mean that one should abandon gain scores altogether (Rogosa and Willett, 1983).

At the workshop, Linn emphasized that although it is important to recognize the uncertainty due to measurement error at the individual student level, value-added models focus on aggregate results—average results for a group of students linked to a certain teacher, school, or educational program. Consequently, the magnitude of the measurement error associated with a group mean, as well as the corresponding reliability, is most relevant to an evaluation of the results of value-added results. Because errors of measurement at the individual student level may be correlated, the variability of the errors of measurement for group means are not simply the sum of the variances associated with individual student errors of measurement. More to the point, the reliability of group average scores may be higher or lower than the reliability of the individual scores that are used to compute that average[3] (Zumbo and Forer, 2008). Brennan, Yin, and Kane (2003) examined this issue using data from the Iowa Tests of Basic Skills. They investigated the dependability of district-level differences in mean scores from one year to the next and found that the degree of uncertainty for the mean difference scores was substantial, suggesting that it is important to consider aggregate-level errors in interpreting the results of value-added analyses.

A further complication is that measurement error is not constant along a test score scale. One characteristic of many tests is that measurement error is much higher at the high and low ends of the scale than in the middle. Michael Kolen reported at the workshop that error ratios can be as large as 10 to 1. He speculated that the aggregate score for a school with a large proportion of low-scoring students may include a great deal of measurement error that, in turn, may have a substantial effect on the accuracy of its value-added estimates.

---

[3]The explanation has to do with the fact that reliability is directly related to the ratio of the variance of the measurement error to the variance in the true scores. Ordinarily, taking averages reduces both variances, so that it is not clear a priori whether their ratio increases or decreases.

Measurement Error and the Stability of Teacher Effects

As long as some measurement error is specific to individuals, measurement error is greater when aggregate test scores are based on a smaller rather than a larger number of students' test scores. Small sample sizes are particularly a problem when trying to estimate teacher effects. For a given school, there are more students at the school than teachers (although there are some very small schools in rural areas). Because longitudinal student data are needed, missing data can further shrink the sample size. For a classroom of 25 students, the effective sample size may dwindle down to 10 because of missing data and student mobility.

Ballou (2005) studied the stability of teacher rankings derived from Tennessee's value-added model in 1998 and 1999 for elementary and middle school teachers in a moderately large school district. He found that 40 percent of the mathematics teachers whose estimated teacher effects ranked in the bottom quartile in 1998 were also in the bottom quartile in 1999; however, 30 percent of those teachers ranked above the median in 1999. Although stability was somewhat better for teachers who ranked in the top quartile in 1998, "nearly a quarter of those who were in the top quartile in 1998 dropped below the median the following year" (Ballou, 2005, p. 288). Such fluctuations can be due to measurement error and other sources of imprecision, as well as changes in the context of teaching from year to year. A high level of instability is a problem for using the estimated teacher effects in a given year for high-stakes teacher accountability. Employing a "three year rolling average" of estimated value-added is a commonly used remedy.

Interval Scales

Many value-added models are elaborate regression models and, as such, the data must meet certain technical assumptions. One of the main assumptions is that the test scores in the analyses are represented on an equal-interval scale (Ballou, 2008; Reardon and Raudenbush, 2008). With an interval scale, equal-sized gains at all points on the scale represent the same increment of test performance. It is clear that a number of scales that are used to report test scores, such as percentile ranks or grade-equivalent scores, are not equal-interval scales. Floor and ceiling effects also militate against the equal interval property.[4]

Scales developed using item response theory (IRT, a psychometric theory currently used to score most standardized tests) are sometimes

---

[4]Floor and ceiling effects may prove to be problematic when measuring growth across grades.

claimed to be equal interval, but the claim is controversial and cannot be easily verified. Furthermore, even if IRT produces such interval scales, it does so according to a particular way of measuring that does not necessarily correspond to the values society places on differences in the intervals. For example, temperature is an equal interval scale, in the sense that it takes an equal amount of energy to increase the temperature of an object by one degree, regardless of its current temperature. However, it is not an interval scale for "comfortableness." Raising the temperature from 60° Fahrenheit to 70° affects comfort differently than raising it from 90° to 100°. Similarly, even if the IRT scale has equal intervals based on some definition, it is unlikely to have equal intervals based on the value society places on improvements at different points on the scale.

At the same time, it must be acknowledged that, in the social sciences, the strict requirement of an equal-interval scale is honored much more in the breach than in the observance. At a practical level, the issue comes down to the impact of departures from this assumption on the validity of the inferences based on the statistical results. This is particularly germane (and problematic) in the context of value-added analysis, which typically demands score scales that extend over several grades. Such scales are constructed through a procedure called "vertical linking."

Vertical Scales

Reckase explained that when the left side of the model (the criterion) is a gain score rather than a test score for a single point in time, the measurement requirements are more stringent. Gain scores are supposed to provide a measure of growth from one testing occasion to the next. Computing gain scores makes sense only when the two measures are comparable—that is, when the two tests measure the same constructs (with approximately the same emphasis) and use the same units of measurement in such a way that results can reasonably be represented on the same interval scale. Of course, there are many reasons to want to use different measures—tests that are used at the end of one grade are generally not suitable for use at the end of the next grade, because students at the higher grade have been learning content appropriate for the higher grade and the test needs to reflect that content. But there must be coherence across the sets of knowledge and skills measured at each grade when test scores are to be used for value-added analysis, whether or not gain scores are used explicitly.

Most approaches to value-added analysis require a vertical score scale that spans a consecutive sequence of grades and allows the estimation of student growth along a continuum (Young, 2006). Under ideal conditions, vertical scales allow users to compare a student's scale score in one grade with that student's scale score in another grade, in order to quantify his or her progress. In the statistical process called vertical linking, the tests are "linked" by including some of the same questions on tests for different grades, so that a few of the same questions appear, for example, on both the third grade and fourth grade test forms, and a few of the same questions appear on both the fourth grade and fifth grade tests, and so on, through the span of grades. Data from the responses to the questions that are common from one grade to the next are then used to construct the vertical scale. However, as noted above, the validity of the inferences based on the analysis of test data represented on a vertical scale depends in part on how closely the vertical scale satisfies the equal-interval scale criterion. Although there was a range of opinions expressed at the workshop, many of the measurement experts on the panel expressed serious concerns on this point—particularly if the linking spans several grades.

Tests that are constructed for use at different grade levels are not strictly equivalent, in the sense that two forms of the SAT might be considered to be. Thus, the linkage between tests designed for use at different grades is necessarily weaker than the equating that is done between test forms intended to be parallel, such as those used at the same grade or for tests like the SAT (Linn, 1993; Mislevy, 1992). The nature of the linkage affects the psychometric properties of the vertical scale and, consequently, can have a substantial impact on teacher and school effects that result from the value-added model. Again, it has proven difficult to judge the degree of distortion in a particular context.

The tests used at different grade levels obviously differ by design in both difficulty and content coverage, paralleling changes in the curriculum from grade to grade. Moreover, the relative emphasis on different construct dimensions changes across grade levels. For example, according to the Mathematics Content Standards for California Public Schools (California State Board of Education, 1997), by the end of fourth grade, students are expected to understand large numbers and addition, subtraction, multiplication, and division of whole numbers, as well as be able to compare simple fractions and decimals. By the end of fifth grade, students should increase their facility with the four basic arithmetic operations applied to fractions, decimals, and positive and negative numbers. The common questions that are used for the vertical linking may perform differently across grades. For example, a question that requires manipulation of complex fractions may be appropriate for a fifth grade test but may reflect content that has not been taught to most fourth graders. In one grade, the responses may reflect actual learning; in the other, they may represent guessing. That is, the mix of response styles to the common questions will generally be different in the two grades. It is not apparent what the effect of these differences is on the properties of the resulting vertical scale.

A related issue is how test design choices impact the vertical scales and, ultimately, the value-added estimates. Schmidt, Houang, and McKnight (2005) showed that constructing a vertically linked test battery may lead to more emphasis on knowledge and skills that are common across grades and less emphasis on relatively unique material specific to any given grade. Such a focus on certain parts of a subject domain while neglecting others can lead to bias in the estimation of school or teacher effectiveness, and perhaps, more importantly, create incentives for teachers to target their instruction on particular subdomains, neglecting others that are equally important. Schmidt and colleagues also concluded that vertical scales make the tests relatively insensitive to instruction, because the common items used in these scales represent abilities that accrue over time, rather than the kinds of knowledge and skills that are most directly associated with a particular teaching experience. Martineau (2006) found that the changing definition of the construct across grades, accompanied by changes in the weights of the different components of the construct across the sequence of tests, can have serious implications for the validity of the score inferences derived from the vertical scales. Again, there is some difference of opinion on the seriousness of the problem in real-world situations.

Other researchers have focused on different approaches to constructing vertical scales and how they can result in different value-added estimates. Briggs, Weeks, and Wiley (2008) constructed eight different vertical scales for the same set of tests at consecutive grade levels. The approaches differed with respect to the IRT model used, the method used to estimate student scale scores, and the IRT calibration method used to place items from the different grades on the vertical scale. Although the estimated school effects from the value-added analyses were highly correlated for the eight vertical scales, the estimated school effects differed for the different scales. The researchers found that the numbers of schools that could be reliably classified as effective, average, or ineffective was somewhat sensitive to the choice of the underlying vertical scale. This is of some concern as there is no "best" approach to vertical scaling. Indeed, the choice of vertical scaling methodology, unlike test content, is not specified by contract and is usually decided by the test vendor. Tong and Kolen (2007) found that the properties of vertical scales, including the amount of average year-to-year growth and within-grade variability, were quite sensitive to how the vertical scale was constructed. Thus, caution is needed when interpreting school, teacher, or program effects from value-added modeling because estimated performance will depend on both the particular skills that are measured by the tests and the particular vertical scaling method used. Despite these problems, the use of a well-constructed vertical scale may yield results that provide a general sense of the amount of growth that has taken place from grade to grade.

If vertical scales are to be used, regular checks are important to make sure that scaling artifacts are not driving the results. For example, one should be suspicious of results that suggest that teachers serving low-ability students are generally obtaining the largest value-added estimates. If there is suspicion of a ceiling effect, then one can check whether teacher rankings change if only the lowest half of each class is used for the analysis.

Model of Learning

In his presentation, Doug Willms stated that "added value is about student learning. Therefore, any discussion of added value needs to begin with some model of what learning entails, and its estimation requires an explicit model of learning" (Willms, 2008, p. 1). He went on to explain that there are critical transitions in learning. For example, all points on the reading scale are not created equal. There is a critical transition from "learning to read" to "reading to learn," which for most students occurs around age 8, typically by the end of third grade. Willms explained that "if children are not able to read with ease and understand what they have read when they enter fourth grade, they are less able to take advantage of the learning opportunities that lie ahead" (p. 5). For good reasons one may want to acknowledge schools that are effective in moving children across that transition. Value-added models might be used to identify schools, teachers, or programs that are most successful in moving children across that transition in a timely fashion and give credit for it (using an ordinal scale that identifies key milestones). Indeed, some transitions can be accorded extra credit because of their perceived importance.

Kolen made a similar point regarding the development of vertically scaled tests. If vertical scales are to become more widely used in the future, he argued that content standards will need to be better articulated within and across grades to lend themselves to measuring growth and vertical scaling. Such articulation would make it clear which content standards are assessed at each grade and which content standards overlap across grades. Such well-articulated standards could then be used in test design and the construction of a vertical scale that captures the "right" intervals on an interval scale, that correspond to the values society places on improvements at different points on the scale. In principle, one could use this scale to design an incentive system that focuses on getting students across critical transition points. But even this scale would only be "right" with respect to this particular criterion. It would not be the right measure of how hard it is to move a student from one level to another, and the model derived from this scale would probably not do a good job of measuring who the best teachers are in this respect. In general, of two teachers beginning the year with otherwise similar students at level 1, one would prefer the teacher who brought more to level 2, but one would not know whether this teacher was better or worse than one who began and ended the year with students at level 3.

This discussion suggests that in order to make value-added models more useful, improved content standards are needed that lay out developmental pathways of learning and highlight critical transitions; tests could then be aligned to such developmental standards. This would improve all models that use prior test scores to predict current performance and would be particularly helpful for those that measure growth using gain scores. Several reports by the National Research Council (2001, 2005, 2007a, 2007b) summarize recent developments in the areas of learning progressions and trajectories.

Key Research Areas

A number of important test-related issues need to be resolved before policy makers can have justifiable confidence in value-added results for high-stakes decisions. Key research questions discussed at the workshop include

- What are the effects of measurement error on the accuracy of the estimates of teacher, school, or program effects? What is the contribution of measurement error to the volatility in estimates over time (e.g., a teacher's value-added estimates over a number of years)?
- Since there are questions about the assumption that test score scales are equal-interval, to what extent are inferences from value-added modeling sensitive to monotonic transformations (meaning transformations that preserve the original order) of test scores?
- Given the problems described above, how might value-added analyses be given a thorough evaluation prior to operational implementation? One way of evaluating a model is to generate simulated data that have the same characteristics as operational data and determine whether the model can accurately capture the relationships that were built into the simulated data. If the model does not estimate parameters with sufficient accuracy from data that are generated to fit the model and match the characteristics of the test data, then there is little likelihood that the model will work well with actual test data. Note that doing well by this measure

is necessary but not sufficient to justify use of the value-added model.

CONCLUSION

Different workshop participants tended to identify many of the same measurement issues associated with value-added models. As Linn observed, at this time these are "problems without much in the way of solutions."

Discussant Kevin Lang asked the measurement presenters, "How many of these issues are unique to VAM; that is, how many of these are also problems with current accountability systems?" Linn explained that many of the problems are present now in test-based accountability systems under NCLB, such as issues about how well the tests reflect the most valued educational goals. However, the vertical scale issues and the equal interval assumption are more specific to VAM applications. As far as measurement error, Linn said, "I guess one difference is that the VAM has this kind of scientific aura about it, and so it's taken to be more precise."

According to Kolen, there are several critical questions: Are estimated teacher and school effects largely due to idiosyncrasies of statistical methods, measurement error, the particular test examined, and the scales used? Or are the estimated teacher and school effects due at least in part to educationally relevant factors? He argued that these questions need to be answered clearly before a value-added model is used as the sole indicator to make important educational decisions.

4

Analytic Issues

Analysts use a variety of methods to estimate value-added effects. All value-added models (VAMs) adjust for students' starting level of achievement using prior test scores, but they do so in different ways. Some also adjust for student characteristics and school context variables. The outcome of applying any model is that some schools, teachers, or programs are identified as being significantly better or worse than average. The models differ in the number of years of data they use, the kinds of assumptions they make, how they handle missing data, and so on. Not surprisingly, findings may differ depending on the model chosen and how it is specified.

This chapter begins with a review of some major challenges with these analytic methods—including nonrandom assignment of teachers and students, bias, precision, stability, data quality, and the balance between complexity and transparency—and causal interpretations. That is followed by a brief overview of two broad approaches to value-added modeling and the strengths and limitations of each. It concludes with a discussion about areas in which further research is most needed, as well as a summary of the main messages that emerged from the workshop regarding analytic approaches.

ANALYTIC CHALLENGES FOR VALUE-ADDED MODELING

Nonrandom Assignment of Teachers and Students

A primary goal of value-added modeling is to make causal inferences by identifying the component of a student's test score trajectory that can be credibly associated with a particular teacher, school, or program. In other words, the purpose is to determine how students' achievement differs, having been in their assigned school, teacher's classroom, or program, from what would have been observed had they been taught in another school, by another teacher, or in the absence of the program. This is often referred to as the estimation of *counterfactual quantities*—for example, the expected outcomes for students taught by teacher A had they been taught by teacher B and vice versa.

The ideal research design for obtaining evidence about effectiveness is one in which students are randomly assigned to schools, teachers, or programs. With random assignment and sufficiently large samples, differences in achievement among schools, teachers, or programs can be directly estimated and inferences drawn regarding their relative effectiveness. However, in the real world of education, random assignment is rarely possible or even desirable. There are many ways that classroom assignments depart from randomness, and some are quite purposeful (e.g., matching individual students' to teachers' instructional styles).[1] Different schools and teachers often serve very different student populations, and programs are typically targeted at particular groups of students, so straightforward comparisons may be neither fair nor useful.

As workshop presenter Dale Ballou explained, to get around the problem of nonrandom assignment, value-added models adjust for preexisting differences among students using their starting levels of achievement. Sometimes a gain score model is used, so the outcome measure is students' growth from their own starting point a year prior; sometimes prior achievement is included as a predictor or control variable in a regression or analysis of covariance; and some models use a more extensive history of student test scores as control variables, as in William Sanders's work.

Many researchers believe that controlling for students' prior achievement is not enough—that more needs to be done to statistically adjust for differences between the groups of students assigned to different schools, teachers, or programs. That is, the question is whether the test score history incorporated into the model is sufficient to account for differences among students on observed—and unobserved (e.g., systematic differences in

---

[1]Random assignment provides information about the relative effectiveness of the teacher with a randomly assigned set of students. There are many reasons that this might not reveal the parameter of policy interest in a world in which students are not randomly assigned.

student motivation or parent support at home)—characteristics that are statistically associated with academic achievement. Ballou explained that nontest-score characteristics can be associated with students' rates of gain in achievement, but relatively few of them are typically measured and available in education data sets. Some variables associated with achievement are generally available, such as students' socioeconomic status, gender, or race. Other contextual factors are more difficult to quantify, such as home environment and peer influences, as well as various school characteristics.

Another problem is that educational inputs are generally conflated, so a classroom of students might receive inputs from the school administration, the teacher, other teachers in the school, the community, and other students in the classroom, many of which are related and overlap to some extent. For example, although a value-added model may purport to be estimating the effect of an individual teacher, adjusting for differences in student backgrounds and prior achievement, this estimate may also be confounded with (i.e., "picking up") unmeasured contextual variables, such as the contributions of the school's leadership, the quality of a teacher's colleagues, and other factors. The contributions of these factors, positive or negative, may end up being attributed to the teacher.

Dan McCaffrey noted that most statistical models that have been used in practice have tended *not* to include student- or context-level predictor variables, such as race or socioeconomic status measures. One argument for excluding such covariates is that including them might imply different expectations for students of different sociodemographic classes. Another concern is that if a certain racial group is exposed to poorer teachers, the model could inappropriately attribute lower performance to race rather than to teacher quality.[2] However, there are also technical challenges to including such variables in the model. Ballou, Sanders, and Wright (2004) investigated the effects of including these types of student-level covariates in the models that avoided the technical problems; the researchers found that their inclusion had no appreciable effect on estimates of classroom effects. However, attempts to expand the methods to include classroom-level variables resulted in unstable estimates (Ballou, 2005).

Bias

Bias refers to the inaccuracy of an estimate that is due to a shortcoming or incompleteness in a statistical model itself. For example, imagine a value-added model focused on isolating the effectiveness of schools using school-wide test results. Suppose that the fourth grade

---

[2]This is more of a potential problem with random-effects than fixed-effects models; see page 50 for an explanation of these models.

test is a gateway test. In schools with advantaged children, large numbers of parents enroll their children in private test preparation sessions in advance of the exam, while parents of children in other schools do not. Students in the first group would tend to perform better on the test than would be predicted on the basis of the third grade test. Even if all schools provided instruction of equal quality, value-added estimates would indicate that the schools serving the first group were more effective, even though they were not responsible for the higher performance of their students. In this case, the estimates would be biased because the contributions of the private test preparation sessions are confounded with true school effectiveness. One way to address this bias would be to augment the model in such a way as to include outside test preparation as a variable (Organisation for Economic Co-operation and Development, 2008). Addition of more student background and context variables to a value-added model can reduce bias but can also lead to more complications, such as missing data.

The prior example illustrated the problem of *underadjustment* in the model. There is also the potential for the reverse problem of *overadjustment*. To continue the previous example, suppose that the fifth grade test is not a gateway test, and therefore parents in schools with advantaged children do not use tutoring. Now, children in these schools do less well on the fifth grade test than predicted based on their (test preparation inflated) fourth grade scores. Similarly, if the children in the advantaged schools do well on both the third and fourth grade tests, in part because such schools are able to hire better teachers, then, depending on the approach used, the model may attribute too much of the high fourth grade scores to the "quality of the students" reflected in the third grade scores and too little to the quality of the fourth grade teachers.

Finally, Ballou and a few others raised the issue that current value-added models assume that there is a single teacher effect that is common for all students. Yet one can readily imagine that one teacher might work very effectively with struggling students but not really be able to stimulate students already performing at high levels, and the opposite might be true of another teacher. Value-added models usually attempt to summarize a teacher's effectiveness in a single number. If teacher quality is multidimensional in this sense, then frequently it will not be possible to say that one teacher is better than another because of the scaling issues discussed in Chapter 3. The importance of this problem depends on the goal of the model. If the objective is to rank all teachers, the problem is likely to be very serious. If the goal is to create incentives to teach struggling students well, the problem may be less serious.

Precision

The precision of the estimated effects is also an important issue. The precision problem differs from the bias problem in that it stems, in large part, from small sample sizes. Small sample sizes are more of a challenge for value-added models that seek to measure teacher effects rather than school effects. This is because estimates of school effects tend to be derived from test score data of hundreds of students, whereas estimates of teacher effects are often derived from data for just a few classes. (Elementary teachers may teach just one class of students each year, whereas middle and high school teachers may have more than 100 students in a given year.) If the number of students per teachers is low, just a few poorly performing students can lower the estimate of a teacher's effectiveness substantially. Research on the precision of value-added estimates consistently finds large sampling errors. As McCaffrey reported, based on his prior research (McCaffrey et al., 2005), standard errors are often so large that about two-thirds of estimated teacher effects are not statistically significantly different from the average.

Stability

A related problem is the stability of estimates. All value-added models produce estimates of school or teacher effects that vary from year to year. This raises the question of the degree to which this instability reflects real variation in performance from year to year, rather than error in the estimates. McCaffrey discussed research findings (Aaronson, Barrows, and Sanders, 2007; Ballou, 2005) demonstrating that only about 30 to 35 percent of teachers ranked in either the top or bottom quintile in one year remain there in the next year. If estimates were completely random, 20 percent would remain in the same quintile from one year to the next. If the definition of a weak teacher is one in the bottom quintile, then this suggests that a significant proportion of teachers identified as weak in a single year would be falsely identified. In another study, McCaffrey, Sass, and Lockwood (2008) investigated the stability of teacher effect estimates from one year and cohort of students to the next (e.g., the estimated teacher effect estimates in 2000-2001 compared to those in 2001-2002) for elementary and middle school teachers in four counties in Florida. They computed 12 correlations (4 counties by 3 pairs of years) for elementary school teachers and 16 correlations (4 counties by 4 pairs of years) for middle school teachers. For elementary school teachers, the 12 correlations between estimates in consecutive years ranged from .09 to .34 with a median of .25. For middle school teachers, the 16 correlations ranged from .05 to .35 with a median of .205. Thus, the year-to-year stability of estimated teacher effects can be characterized as being quite low from one year to the next.

Instability in value-added estimates is not only a result of sampling error due to the small numbers of students in classes. McCaffrey and his colleagues (2008) found that the year-to-year variability in teacher effects exceeded what might be expected from simple sampling error. This year-to-year variability generally accounted for a much larger share of the variation in effects for elementary school teachers than for middle school teachers (perhaps because middle school teachers usually tend to teach many more students in a single year than elementary teachers). Further, year-to-year variability was only weakly related to teachers' qualifications, such as their credentials, tenure status, and annual levels of professional development. Whether this variability reflects real changes in teachers' performance or a source of error at the classroom level (such as peer effects that are usually omitted from the model) remains unknown.

Instability will tend to erode confidence in value-added results on the part of educators because most researchers and education practitioners will expect that true school, teacher, or even program performance will change only gradually over time rather than display large swings from year to year. Moreover, if estimates are unstable, they will not be as credible for motivating or justifying changes in future behavior or programs. One possible solution would be to consider several years' of data when making important decisions, such as teacher tenure.

Data Quality

Missing or faulty data can have a negative impact on the precision and stability of value-added estimates and can contribute to bias. The procedures used to transform the raw test data into usable data files, as well as the completeness of the data, should be carefully evaluated when deciding whether to use a value-added model. Student records for two or more years are needed, and it is not uncommon in longitudinal data files for some scores to be missing because of imperfect record matching, student absences, and students transferring into or out of a school.

A key issue for implementing value-added methods is the capacity to link students to their teachers. As Helen Ladd noted, many state data systems do not currently provide direct information on which students are taught by which teachers. Ladd stated, "Until recently, for example, those of us using the North Carolina data have had to make inferences about a student's teacher from the identity of the proctor of the relevant test and a wealth of other information from school activity reports. In my own work, I have been able to match between 60-80 percent of students to their teachers at the elementary and high school levels but far lower percentages at the middle school level" (Ladd, 2008, p. 9). She went on to say that even if states start providing more complete data of this type, a number of issues still complicate the situation—for example, how to deal with students who are pulled out of their regular classes for part of the day, team-taught courses, and students who transfer into or out of a class in the middle of the year. Attributing learning to a certain school or teacher is difficult in systems in which there is high student mobility. Moreover, if the reason that the data are missing is related to test score outcomes, the resulting value-added estimates can be seriously biased.

Generally, the greater the proportion of missing data, the weaker the credibility of the value-added results. Of course, missing data are a problem for any type of test score analysis, but some models depend on student- or context-level characteristics, which may be especially incomplete. The integrity and completeness of such data need to be evaluated before implementing a value-added system. When value-added models are used for research purposes or program evaluation, the standard for what constitutes sufficient data may be somewhat lower than when the purpose is for school or teacher improvement or for accountability. Ladd emphasized this point, noting that if these models are to be used as part of a teacher evaluation system, capturing only 60-80 percent of the student data probably will not be sufficient; it may not be possible to include all teachers in the analysis.

Finally, there is the problem that very large numbers of teachers would not have test score data for computing value-added scores. Many subjects and grades are not currently assessed using large-scale tests, so most K-2 and high school teachers, as well as teachers of such subjects as social studies, foreign languages, physical education, and arts are not directly linked to state-level student test scores. This presents a major obstacle to implementing a value-added evaluation system of teachers at a district level. (This problem applies to using status test score data for teacher evaluation as well.)

Complexity Versus Transparency

Value-added models range from relatively simple regression models to extremely sophisticated models that require rich databases and state-of-the-art computational procedures. McCaffrey and Lockwood (2008) suggest that "complex methods are likely to be necessary for accurate estimation of teacher effects and that accountability or compensation systems based on performance measures with weak statistical properties will fail to provide educators with useful information to guide their practice and could eventually erode their confidence in such systems" (p. 10). However, there is always a limit, beyond which adding complexity to the analysis results in little or no advantages. When used for purposes such as accountability, the choice of models needs to balance the goals of complexity and accuracy, on one hand, and transparency, on the other. At the same time, it is likely that the importance attached to transparency will depend on other features of the accountability system of which the value-added model is but one component, as well as the political context in which the accountability system is operating.

Transparency refers to the ability of educators and the public to understand how the estimates were generated and what they mean. A major goal of improvement and accountability systems is to provide educators with signals about what is considered effective performance and whether they have achieved it, as well as to motivate lower performing individuals to change their behavior to improve their effectiveness. There is general agreement that highly complex statistical procedures are difficult for educators to understand, which leads to a concern that the use of such procedures might limit the practical utility of value-added models. Workshop participant Robert Gordon raised the issue of whether many of the models are simply "too esoteric to be useful to teachers in the real world." This is an important consideration when these models are used for accountability because a key aspect of their success is acceptance by teachers and administrators. In contrast, when the models are used for research or program evaluation, transparency may not be important.

Transparency also may not be an overriding concern for public uses, such as for accountability. Henry Braun recounted a discussion with policy makers who judged that transparency was important but not crucial. These policy makers indicated that they did not need to know the details of what went into the "black box" to produce value-added results. If the results were trustworthy and the rationale could be explained in an understandable way, they believed that school systems would be willing to forgo transparency for the sake of accuracy. For example, most current tests are scored using item response theory, which is also very complex. However, test users generally accept the reported test scores, even though they do not fully understand the mathematical intricacies through which they are derived (i.e., the process for producing raw scores, scale scores, and equating the results to maintain year-to-year comparability). Analysis raw scores are converted to scale scores and then further adjusted through an equating process to maintain year-to-year comparability.

A key consideration in the trade-off between complexity and transparency is the resources required to implement the more complex models. Complex models require greater technical expertise on the part of staff. It is critical that the staff conducting sophisticated analyses have the expertise to run them correctly and interpret the results appropriately. Complex models also usually require more comprehensive data. Data availability and data quality, as described in the previous section, place limits on the complexity of the models that can be considered. Thus, a number of issues have to be weighed to achieve the optimal balance between complexity, accuracy, and transparency when choosing a value-added model.

Causal Interpretations

Although not always stated explicitly, the goal of value-added modeling is to make causal inferences. In practical terms, this means drawing conclusions, such as that certain teachers caused the higher (or lower) achievement in their students.

The two disciplines that focus on value-added modeling take different approaches to this problem. The statistics discipline generally handles it by characterizing its models as *descriptive*, not causal; however, it does recognize that using such models to evaluate schools, teachers, or programs implicitly treats the results as causal effects. Lockwood and McCaffrey (2007) identify conditions under which the estimates derived from statistical models approximate causal effects. The economics discipline generally makes certain assumptions that, if met, support causal interpretations of value-added results obtained from the models it favors. The critical assumption is that any differences among classes, schools, or programs that are not captured by the predictor variables used in the model are captured by the student fixed-effect components. In the end, despite their status as empirical descriptions, the results of the statistical models are used in ways similar to the econometric models—that is, to support causal interpretations.

Rothstein (2009) tested the assumptions of the economics models in the context of estimating teacher effects in North Carolina. His idea was to see if estimated teacher effects can predict the achievement gains of their students in the years prior to these students being in their classes. For example, does a fifth grade teacher effect predict her students' achievement gains when those students were third and fourth graders? Indeed, he found that, for example, fifth grade teachers were nearly as strongly linked statistically to their students' fourth grade scores as were the students' fourth grade teachers. Rothstein also found that the relationship between current teachers and prior gains differs by time span: that is, the strength of the statistical association of the fifth grade teacher with fourth grade gains differs from that with third grade gains.

Since teachers cannot rewrite the past, the finding that teachers' effects predict their students' prior performance implies there is selection of students into teachers' classrooms that is related to student prior achievement growth and other dynamic factors, not simply to time-invariant characteristics of the students. The implication is that, in such settings, the central assumption of the econometric model does not hold and value-added estimates are likely to be biased. The size of the bias and the prevalence of the conditions leading to the violations are unknown. Although Rothstein's study was intended to test the specification of the econometric models, it has important implications for the interpretation of estimates from statistical models as well, because dynamic classroom assignment would also violate the assumptions that Lockwood and McCaffrey (2007) establish for allowing causal interpretation of statistical model estimates. Analysts in both paradigms have been taken aback by Rothstein's (2009) results. Some researchers are currently conducting studies to see whether they will replicate Rothstein's findings; if Rothstein's findings are confirmed, then both camps may need to adapt their modeling approaches to address the problematic aspects of their current assumptions (McCaffrey and Lockwood, 2008).

TWO MAIN ANALYTIC APPROACHES

A full explication of value-added analytic methods is too complex to include in this report. Nontechnical readers may want to skip the relatively brief explanation of the two main analytic approaches that follows, because it assumes some statistical background and is not essential for understanding the rest of the report. Readers who are interested in more technical information are referred to the workshop transcript and background papers (available at http://www7.nationalacademies.org/bota/VAM_Workshop_Agenda.html), as well as Graham, Singer, and Willett (in press); Harris and Sass (2005); McCaffrey and Lockwood (2008); McCaffrey et al. (2003); Organisation for Economic Co-operation and Development (2008); and Willett and Singer (in preparation).

Simplifying somewhat, there are two general choices to be made in the design and estimation of value-added models. (To make matters concrete, we focus this discussion on obtaining value-added scores for teachers.) The first choice concerns how to adjust for differences among students taught by different teachers. The second choice concerns the estimation methodology.

One approach to adjusting for student differences is to incorporate into the model a parameter for each student (i.e., student fixed effects). The student fixed effects include, for a given student, all the unobservable characteristics of the student and family (including community context) that contribute to achievement and are stable across time (McCaffrey and Lockwood, 2008). Advocates of using student fixed effects argue that measured student covariates are unlikely to remove all the relevant differences among students of different teachers. For example, in a comparison of students with the same prior test scores, a student in the more advantaged school is likely to differ from a student in a less advantaged school on a number of other characteristics related to academic achievement. If they are both performing at the national 50th percentile, the student at the less advantaged school may exhibit more drive to overcome disadvantages. Using student fixed effects captures all unchanging (time-invariant) student characteristics and thus eliminates selection bias stemming from the student characteristics not included in the model, provided that the model is otherwise properly specified.

But elimination of this bias may come at a significant cost. Because it requires estimation of a coefficient for each student, it will generally make estimation of the other coefficients less reliable (have higher variance). Thus, there is a trade-off between bias and variance that may favor one choice or the other. In addition, when fixed effects are used, it is impossible to compare groups of teachers whose students do not commingle at some point. For example, if students at school A always start and end their school careers there, as do students at school B, by using fixed effects, one can never tell whether students do better at school A because they are more advantaged or because school A has better teachers. Even when the students do overlap, the estimates rely heavily on the outcomes for students changing schools, generally a small fraction of the total student population. This, too, reduces the reliability of estimates using fixed student effects. Because the students who change schools are not likely to be representative of the student population, biased estimates can result.[3] Which approach produces lower mean-squared error depends on the specifics of the problem.

A similar set of issues arises when deciding whether to estimate teacher value-added as the coefficient on a teacher fixed effect or through the formulation of a random-effects model. Employing random-effects estimates can introduce bias because it may attribute to the student some characteristics that are common to teachers in the school. If advantaged children tend to have better teachers, with random effects one will attribute some of the benefit of having better teachers to being advantaged and will predict higher test scores for these children than they would actually achieve with average teachers. This, in turn, will make their teachers appear to have provided less value-added. In contrast, incorporating teacher fixed effects would eliminate this source of bias.[4]

---

[3]Note that differential student mobility across schools or teachers can lead to nonrandom changes in the contexts of teaching and learning that are not captured by the model and thus can introduce bias into the estimates of value-added.

[4]From a technical perspective, a necessary condition for a model employing teacher random effects to yield unbiased estimates is that teachers' effectiveness is uncorrelated with student characteristics. The example in the text offers a case in which this condition does not hold.

Advocates of using random effects for teachers respond that this seeming advantage of the fixed-effects approach depends on the model being otherwise specified correctly; that is, all the other variables contributing to student outcomes are properly represented in the model. If the model is seriously misspecified, then fixed-effects estimates may well be more biased than random-effects estimates. Moreover, the fixed-effects estimates tend to be quite volatile, especially when the number of students linked to a teacher is small. In general, random-effects estimates will have lower variance but higher bias than fixed-effects estimates.[5] Either could have lower mean-squared error. The smaller number of parameters estimated in the random-effects model also makes it easier to include more complexity. Thus, the appropriateness of a model will always depend in some measure on the particular context of use and, for this reason, there was little optimism that a particular approach to estimating value-added would be always preferred.

A final decision is whether to "shrink" the estimates. To some extent, this decision reflects whether one comes, like most econometricians, from a "frequentist" statistical tradition or, like most modern statisticians, a "Bayesian" statistical tradition. If one thinks that nothing is known about the distribution of teacher effects (the frequentist approach), then the estimate derived from the model (usually the fixed effect) is the best estimate of the teacher effect. However, if one thinks something is known about this distribution (the Bayesian approach), then a very large positive or negative (usually random effect) estimate of the teacher effect is unlikely and is probably the result of random errors. Therefore, the estimates should be shrunk toward the mean. The two approaches can be reconciled by using the estimated distribution of teacher effects to infer the actual distribution of teacher effects. This approach, known as "empirical Bayes," is quite complex. If all teacher effects are estimated with the same precision, then shrinking does not change the ranking of teachers, only their score. If there is more information on some teachers, then those on whom there is less information will have less precisely estimated teacher effects, and these estimated effects will be shrunk more. Such teachers will rarely be found in the extreme tails of the distribution of value-added estimates.

---

[5]In the most common formulations of random-effects models, estimates of teacher value-added are pulled toward the average (in contrast to estimates based on the data from each teacher alone). For this reason they are often called "shrinkage estimates." The shrinkage reduces variance at the expense of introducing some bias.

Key Research Areas

Workshop participants identified a number of areas in which more research on value-added models is needed in order for researchers, policy makers, and the public to have more confidence in their results. Some key research questions that were discussed at the workshop include

- How might the econometric and statistical models incorporate features from the other paradigm that are missing in their own approaches?
- What are the effects of violations of model assumptions on the accuracy of value-added estimates? For example, what are the effects on accuracy of not meeting assumptions about the assignment of students to classrooms, the characteristics of the missing data, as well as needed sample sizes?
- How do the models perform in simulation studies? One way of evaluating a model is to generate simulated data that have the same characteristics as operational data, but with known parameters, and test whether the model can accurately capture the relationships that were built into the simulated data.
- How could the precision of value-added estimates be improved? Instability declines when multiple years of data are combined, but some research shows that there is true variability in teacher performance across years, suggesting that simply pooling data across years might introduce bias and not allow for true deviation in performance.
- What are the implications of Rothstein's results about causality/bias, for both the economics and the statistical approaches?
- How might value-added estimates of effectiveness be validated? One approach would be to link estimates of school, teacher, or program effects derived from the models with other measures of effectiveness to examine the extent that the various measures concur. Some past studies have looked at whether value-added modeling can distinguish certified and noncertified teachers, in an effort to validate the National Board for Professional Teaching Standards certification. In other words, value-added estimates are treated as the criterion. Another approach would be to turn that on its head and ask: How well do the value-added estimates agree with other approaches to evaluating the relative effectiveness of teachers?
- How do policy makers, educators, and the public use value-added information? What is the appropriate balance between the complex methods necessary for accurate measures and the need for measures to be transparent?

CONCLUSION

Henry Braun summed up the analytic discussion by stating: "To nobody's surprise, there is not one dominant VAM." Each major class of models has shortcomings, there is no consensus on the best approaches, and little work has been done on synthesizing the best aspects of each approach. There are questions about the accuracy and stability of value-added estimates of schools, teachers, or program effects. More needs to be learned about how these properties differ, using different value-added techniques and under different conditions. Most of the workshop participants argued that steps need to be taken to improve accuracy if the estimates are to be used as a primary indicator for high-stakes decisions; rather, value-added estimates should best be used in combination with other indicators. But most thought that the degree of precision and stability does seem sufficient to justify low-stakes uses of value-added results for research, evaluation, or improvement when there are no serious consequences for individual teachers, administrators, or students.

5

Considerations for Policy Makers

The purpose of the workshop was to scan the research on value-added methods to identify their strengths and limitations, which can inform policy makers' decisions about whether and how to proceed with the implementation of these methods in different settings. This chapter summarizes the key policy-relevant messages that emerged from the workshop.

Many participants emphasized that value-added models have the potential to provide useful information for educational decision making, beyond that provided by the test-based indicators that are widely used today. These models are unique in that they are intended to provide credible measures of the contributions of specific teachers, schools, or programs to student test performance. At the same time, participants recognized that there are still many technical and practical issues that need to be resolved in order for researchers to feel confident in supporting certain policy uses of value-added results.

Workshop participants expressed a range of views about the most critical challenges, and the intensity of their concerns varied. Robert Linn expressed concern about overselling by proponents of value-added modeling: "Some think it's the can opener that can open any can. . . . More modest claims are ones that I would endorse." Adam Gamoran and Robert Gordon, among others, focused on what they saw as the advantages of these models over indicators based on student status. Gordon observed that although many important technical issues still need to be resolved, it is not realistic to think that policy makers will wait 20 years until all of the difficulties are worked out before making use of such methods. Decisions about schools and teachers are being made, and, as Jane Hannaway noted, there is enormous demand from the policy side, to which the testing and research communities need to respond as quickly as possible. Some of the technical problems may never be resolved, as is the case with current status models, but many participants asserted that value-added methods can still be used, albeit with caution.

At the same time, throughout the workshop, participants raised a number of questions that they thought were important for policy makers to be asking if they are considering using value-added indicators for evaluation and other purposes.

A RANGE OF VIEWS

Compared to What?

Kevin Lang suggested that, when deciding whether to use value-added methods, one question for decision makers to ask is "Compared to what?" If these models are intended to replace other indicators, will they provide information that is more useful, accurate, or fair than what is currently available? If they are being considered as an additional indicator (in conjunction with others), will the incremental gain in information be substantively meaningful?

Dale Ballou reminded the group that every method for evaluating effectiveness with respect to student achievement (e.g., status, growth, value-added) has risks and rewards. So the question "Compared to what?" is also important to ask about the risk-reward trade-off associated with different test-based evaluation strategies. Many of the concerns about value-added models—including concerns about the models themselves (e.g., transparency and robustness to violations of assumptions), concerns about the test data that feed into the models (e.g., reliability, validity, scaling), and concerns about statistical characteristics of the results (e.g., precision, bias)—also apply to some extent to the assessment models that are currently used by the states. Value-added models do raise some unique issues, which were addressed at the workshop.

Regardless of which evaluation method is chosen, risk is unavoidable. That is, in the context of school accountability, whether decision makers choose to stay with what they do now or to do something different, they are going to incur risks of two kinds: (1) identifying some schools as failing (i.e., truly ineffective) that really are not and (2) neglecting to identify some schools that really are failing. One question is whether value-added models used in place of, or in addition to, other methods will help reduce those risks.

A good strategy when considering the use of a value-added approach is to try not to judge the benefits and drawbacks of various value-added models in isolation. Rather, it would be more appropriate to take a systemic view and think about how a value-added indicator would fit into a particular evaluation system, given the political context, the values of different stakeholders, the types of tests and other data available, and the indicators that will be constructed, as well as the sanctions or rewards to be attached to schools in the different classifications determined by those indicators. Of course, the availability of adequate funding and appropriate expertise also needs to be taken into account. As Sean Reardon and others suggested, this is a design problem: If the overarching challenge is to improve the quality of education for all children, what are the most powerful strategic levers that policy makers can use, given the current situation, and what can be done in the context of measurement, to make the most progress in a cost-effective way? Given the time and expense necessary to carry out a value-added evaluation, is the resulting information more useful for the purpose of educational improvement than the information and indicators currently used—or that provided by other, nonquantitative means?

Dan McCaffrey has conducted some research suggesting that recent implementations of value-added models to improve schooling outcomes have fallen short of expectations. As an example, he cited a pilot program in Pennsylvania in which the information derived from the model was not found by administrators to be very useful—or, at best, of limited additional value compared with the information provided by existing indicators. (However, he noted that these findings were obtained very early in the implementation process.) John Easton described a similar phenomenon in Chicago: essentially the "lack of internal capacity to use [information] profitably," but he nonetheless believes that value-added models can be used for research and evaluation and eventually to identify good school-wide and classroom-based teaching practices.

Is There a Best Value-Added Method?

There are many different types of value-added models, and, to date, no single dominant method. No value-added approach (or any test-based indicator, for that matter) addresses all the challenges to identifying effective or ineffective schools or teachers. As explained in Chapter 4, most workshop participants thought that fixed-effects models generally worked well to minimize the bias that results from selection on fixed (time-invariant) student characteristics, whereas models employing student characteristics and teacher random effects worked well to minimize variance. More needs to be learned about how important properties, such as mean-squared error and stability, vary across different value-added approaches applied in various contexts, as well as the implications of these choices for accountability system design.

Until now, econometricians have favored fixed-effects approaches, and statisticians have used random-effects or mixed-effects approaches.[1] One message from the workshop is that disciplinary traditions should not dictate model choices. Neither approach is best in all situations; one ought to ask which model makes the most sense for the particular research or policy problem being faced, given the data available, and so on.

What Is Needed to Implement a Value-Added Model?

Workshop participants talked about the different capacities that a statewide or district system would need to have in order to properly implement, and to derive meaningful benefits from, a value-added analysis, for example:

- a longitudinal database that tracks individual students over time and accurately links them to their teachers, or at least to schools (if the system will be used only for school and not for teacher accountability);
- confidence that missing data are missing for legitimate reasons (such as student mobility), not because of problems with the data collection system;[2] and
- expert staff to run or monitor the value-added analyses, either in-house or through a contractor.

To maximize the utility of the value-added analysis, some workshop presenters suggested that the system would also need to have

- a vertically coherent set of standards, curriculum and pedagogical strategies that are linked to the standards, and a sequence of tests that it is well aligned to that set of standards (with respect to both content coverage and cognitive complexity);

---

[1]Statisticians use the term "mixed-effects" to denote regression models that incorporate as predictors a set of student characteristics (whose corresponding regression coefficients are treated as fixed) and a set of coefficients representing schools or teachers (and are thought of as being randomly drawn from some distribution). It is unfortunate that the two disciplines sometimes have different meanings for the same term, thereby adding confusion to discussions involving adherents of both traditions.

[2]As discussed in Chapter 4, data missing because of student mobility can introduce bias and increase variability in value-added estimates.

- a reporting system that effectively presents results and provides sufficient support so that users are likely to make appropriate inferences from the analysis;
- an ongoing training program for teachers and administrators, so that they can understand and use the results constructively; and
- a mechanism to monitor and evaluate the model's effects on teachers and students, so the program can be adapted if unintended consequences arise.

It is important to bear in mind that the above are necessary conditions for the optimal use of a value-added analysis. Even if all these capacities were in place, however, technical problems noted in this report, such as those related to bias and precision, would need to be examined prior to implementation for high-stakes purposes.

How High Are the Stakes?

A recurring message throughout the workshop was that value-added models could be useful for low-stakes purposes that do not have serious consequences for individual teachers or schools (such as to help make decisions about professional development needs), but that persistent concerns about precision and bias militate against employing value-added indicators as the principal basis for high-stakes decisions.

One complication is determining exactly what constitutes low versus high stakes. What are low stakes for one person might be high stakes for another. For example, a state official might consider simply reporting school test results to the media, without any sanctions attached to the results, to be low stakes; but a teacher or a principal may feel that such public reporting amounts to high stakes, because it affects her professional reputation and negative results can cause her embarrassment. When there is uncertainty about how different stakeholders will perceive the stakes associated with the results of a value-added system, decision makers should err on the side of assuming that the stakes are high and take the necessary precautions.

The *consequential validity* of an indicator system refers to the appropriateness of actions or uses derived from the test score inferences. Judgments regarding consequential validity can rest on technical analyses, as well as on the examination of both short-term and long-term outcomes. Of course, there may be disagreement among observers about whether the consequences are on the whole positive or negative.

Gordon argued that evidence of the validity of the value-added estimates should be commensurate with the stakes attached. Himself a lawyer, Gordon made a legal analogy.

In the law, we make rules based on our judgments on the relative importance of different interests. We don't like to put innocent people in jail, so
we tip the scales against wrongful convictions. That's why we apply the
beyond reasonable doubt standard in criminal cases. It's why criminal
courts typically refuse to admit polygraph tests. And as a result, we let
guilty people get out of jail. It's not a bug, it's a feature. When the stakes
do not involve the stigma and loss of liberty from a criminal conviction,
we act differently. In civil cases, we just want to get the right answer, so
we apply a preponderance of the evidence standard. That's 50 percent
plus one, and actually courts are more likely . . . to admit polygraphs, because the goal is just to make the right judgment, even if it's just barely.

In other words, the greater the consequences, the greater the burden
on the evidence that is brought to bear. This suggests that, for high-stakes
purposes, there needs to be solid evidence of the reliability and validity
of value-added results—evidence that, in the view of many workshop
participants, is currently not to be had.[3] As discussed below, this view
prompted the idea that value-added models be used in combination with
other accepted indicators of teacher or school performance when making
high-stakes decisions.

Is This a Fair Way to Evaluate Teachers?

Of the various uses to which value-added models could be put, workshop participants expressed a number of concerns regarding their use for
high-stakes decisions affecting individual teachers, such as promotions or
pay. The first problem is that value-added estimates for teachers are usually based on small numbers of students. As discussed in Chapter 3, measurement error tends to be greater when aggregate test scores are based
on a smaller number of students' test scores than when based on a larger
number. Because longitudinal student data are needed, missing data can
further reduce the sample size. Many teachers simply do not teach a large
enough sample of students to be credibly evaluated by a value-added
model. Furthermore, as Lorrie Shepard noted, if high-stakes decisions are
to be made about individual teachers, one would need to provide safe-

---

[3]The *Standards for Educational and Psychological Testing* (American Educational Research
Association, American Psychological Association, and National Council on Measurement in
Education, 1999) emphasize that evidence should be provided of the validity and reliability
of any test use. Test validity refers to the degree to which theory and empirical evidence support the interpretations of test scores entailed by the proposed uses of tests. Reliability refers
to the consistency of measurement when the testing procedure is repeated on a population
of individuals or groups. Current large-scale testing programs, such as those used by states,
routinely document such evidence.

guards, such as data on multiple cohorts of students to determine whether the teacher was, for example, low one year or low three years in a row. Such an approach imposes substantial data requirements.[4]

Second, while any value-added model is almost certainly biased in favor of some groups of teachers and against others, it is usually difficult to determine which ones are which. With status models, which are widely recognized to favor teachers of higher achieving and more advantaged pupils, people frequently make ad hoc adjustments in their interpretation to reflect the known direction of bias. In contrast, with value-added results, not enough is generally known to ascertain the appropriate direction of the correction. In part, this is due to the different sources of confounding that can result in biased estimates.

That said, value-added methods could be useful for lower stakes purposes, such as identifying (apparently) high-performing or low-performing teachers to inform teacher improvement strategies. Brian Stecher suggested that a value-added analysis could provide a preliminary, quantitative indicator to identify certain teachers who might employ pedagogical strategies or exhibit certain behaviors to be emulated, as well as teachers who might need to change their strategies or behaviors. However, statistical analysis alone cannot reveal the specific changes to be made—that requires both direct observation and expertise in pedagogy and professional development. One should certainly be open to the possibility that the evidence gathered in this manner may lead to evaluations that are at odds with those derived from statistical analysis.

How Might Value-Added Modeling Fit into a System of Multiple Measures?

Many workshop presenters favored using value-added models in combination with other measures, particularly when high stakes are attached to the results. As Henry Braun stated, "Even if we are attracted to value-added, and certainly value-added has many advantages over status systems, we are not ready to give up on status."[5] An ideal approach would be to find ways of combining value-added, status, and other types of indicators about teacher, school, or program effectiveness. Doug Willms suggested that additional measures include information about school

---

[4]In discussions of alternatives to value-added analyses, it was pointed out that other approaches (e.g., a principal's observations of a teacher in a classroom) constitute a small sample of the universe of observations that could be made in the course of the school year.

[5]As discussed in earlier chapters, status-based indicators represent specific, content-based milestones for students that are the avowed goals of education. For many observers, these are so essential that, despite their technical shortcomings, they should not be completely supplanted by progress-related measures in the evaluation of schools and teachers.

contextual variables, school process variables, school discipline, and so on. At a minimum, such measures would provide information that could assist in the interpretation of differences among schools or teachers in their value-added results. Mark Wilson pointed out that, in addition to value-added and status models, there is a third alternative: growth (or change) models that do not include value-added adjustments.

There are several ways to combine and report on multiple measures. A school profile report comprises a variety of indicators, usually displayed side by side. Presenting value-added as just one of many indicators could reduce the chance of readers placing too much emphasis on it—or on any other indicator, for that matter. Of course, different observers would focus on different indicators, but the more comprehensive picture would be available and educators would feel that, at least in principle, stakeholders could consider the full range of school outcomes.

In many states, a single index is required and so a rule for combining the indicators must be developed. A simple rule involves standardizing the indicator values and then calculating a weighted average. In a more complex rule, the value of each indicator must exceed a predetermined threshold for a school to avoid sanctions or to be awarded a commendation. For example, the state of Ohio has developed a school rating system that incorporates four measures: (1) graduation and attendance rates, (2) adequate yearly progress under No Child Left Behind, (3) a performance index that combines all test results on a single scale, and (4) a value-added estimate.[6] Schools are placed into one of five categories depending on the values of these indicators in relation to the thresholds.[7]

Scott Marion and Lorrie Shepard described Damian Betebenner's work on the reporting system for Colorado as a good illustration of how status and value-added models might be combined, although this system includes a growth model, not a value-added one. The Colorado Growth Model offers a way for educators to understand how much growth a student made from one year to the next in comparison to his or her academic peers. In many ways, it is similar to a value-added model.[8] The Colorado Growth Model compares each student's performance with students in the same grade throughout the state who had the same sequence of test scores in previous years. The model then produces a (conditional) growth percentile for each student, much like children's height and weight growth charts. A student who grew more than 60 percent of his or her academic

---

[6]For grades 9-12, a growth measure rather than a value-added estimate will be employed.

[7]For more details, see http://www.achieve.org/files/World_Class_Edu_Ohio_FINAL.pdf (pp. 58-59).

[8]Colorado's growth model conditions on all possible prior scores, uses a regression-based estimation procedure, and produces results based on a measure of central tendency.

peers would have a (conditional) growth percentile of 60. Using this model it is possible to determine, in terms of growth percentiles, how much progress a student needs to make to reach proficiency within one, two, or three years.[9]

In addition to calculating and reporting growth results for each student, school, and district, the Colorado Department of Education produces school and district reports depicting both growth and status (percentage proficient and above) results in what has been termed a "four quadrant" report. This report is basically a 2 × 2 figure with growth depicted on the x-axis and divided into those schools (or districts) producing above-average and below-average amounts of student growth. Similarly, the y-axis represents status, in this case in terms of percentage proficient, and divided (arbitrarily) between higher and lower than average status results. This report allows stakeholders to easily see that schools in the lower left quadrant, for example, have lower than average percentages of students achieving proficiency *and* whose students are exhibiting lower than average growth. Such schools might well be considered the highest priority schools for intervention. (To view sample reports, go to http://www.cde.state.co.us/cdeedserv/GrowthCharts-2008.htm.)

Stecher mentioned another approach, which is sometimes referred to as the "triage" strategy. Status and value-added indicators could be used to trigger visits by a team of "inspectors" to conduct a closer evaluation of a school that may be in need of improvement. The point is that test scores cannot tell *why* students' achievement levels and test score trajectories are problematic; trained inspectors might uncover extenuating circumstances or identify specific educational practices that might help. Properly implemented, such a strategy could lead to improvements in school effectiveness. A variant of this approach, involving both quantitative and qualitative measures, is currently being used both in England and in New York City schools.

Hannaway pointed out that there are many levels of decision making in education, and different types of information might be most useful—or politically attractive—at different levels. For example, the federal government might have an accountability system focused primarily on status measures in reading and mathematics. But that does not preclude states and school districts from employing additional indicators that they bring to bear on the allocation of resources or decisions about school viability (as in Ohio, as described above).

---

[9]For a sample report see Colorado Department of Education, http://www.cde.state.co.us/FedPrograms/AYP/download/index_coaypgrowpro.pdf.

How Important Is Transparency?

As discussed in Chapter 4, designers of an evaluation system must consider the trade-off between complexity and transparency. Judith Singer observed that the term transparency was used during the workshop to refer to several different but related ideas: one meaning relates to fairness—people desire a system that is equitable and cannot be "gamed" and that rewards the teachers and schools that truly deserve it. The second meaning relates to methodology—that is, methodologists could "inspect" the model and the estimation machinery in order to evaluate them in relation to professional standards. The third meaning relates to availability of information—that is, providing the public with understandable information about how the methods work. All three seem to be important.

Gordon raised the issue of whether many of the models are simply "too esoteric to be useful to teachers in the real world." Another workshop attendee described his experience implementing value-added models in Chicago and New York. He found that teachers generally understood issues like sample size and random distribution, so the complexity of the models may not necessarily be an overwhelming issue. He felt that teachers would come down on the side of fairness over transparency. That is because they may see status models as unfair, particularly if they have a number of special education students in one year, or because they easily understand that they can have "good" or "bad" batches of students in a given year. "They will go with the more complex models, because the transparent ones they see through easily as being unfair." It is probably most important for stakeholders to understand the logic of using value-added modeling rather than the actual estimation methods.

Another key consideration related to complexity is the resources required to implement the more complex models. Complex models require greater technical expertise on the part of staff. It is critical that the staff conducting sophisticated analyses have the expertise to run them correctly and interpret the results appropriately. These analyses will typically be contracted out, but in-house staff still need to have the expertise to understand and monitor the contractor. Complex value-added models also usually require more comprehensive data, the availability and quality of which places limits on the complexity of the models that can be considered.

How Will the Consequences of Using
Value-Added Models Be Monitored?

Several participants emphasized the importance of monitoring the consequences of using a value-added model to determine its utility in helping states and districts achieve their education goals. When these models are used for real-world purposes, they have consequences, intended and unintended. In the health care example described in Chapter 2, Ashish Jha described how an adjusted status model caused many apparently low-performing surgeons to quit the profession as intended, but also caused some surgeons to turn away high-risk patients, which was unintended. The education field needs to find ways to monitor the impact of value-added models not only on student achievement but also on school policies, instructional practices, teacher morale and mobility, and so on. For example, monitoring the impact on instruction may involve collecting longitudinal data about teacher behaviors, curriculum, and allocation of instructional time across subject areas. Ideally, data collection would begin before implementation of the new system and extend for some years afterward, a substantial undertaking. It is important to allow for flexibility and adaptation over time, as knowledge is accumulated about how the accountability system impacts the larger education system. As Henry Braun commented, "We are dealing with very, very complex systems; there's no reason to believe that we will get it right the first time."

CONCLUSION

Several workshop participants remarked that people should not hold value-added models to higher standards than other measures that are already being widely used for accountability and other high-stakes purposes. All test-based indicators have limitations, and measurement experts have long advised that no single indicator should be the sole basis for high-stakes decisions (National Research Council, 1999). There are well-known problems with the kinds of status models that are now used for accountability. In particular, teachers and schools with more advantaged students will tend to rank higher on status measures than will equally skilled teachers and schools with less advantaged students. It is natural, then, for policy makers and the education community to seek alternatives.

This report conveys some of the advantages that can accrue with the use of value-added models. However, it also presents information about why value-added results are not completely trustworthy. For example, the estimates produced by value-added models are biased (as explained in Chapter 4), and it is difficult to assess the direction and magnitude of the bias. When a school with many disadvantaged students performs at the state average with respect to a status model, most observers would be inclined to judge the school's performance as laudable, although they probably would not do so if the student population were drawn from a very advantaged community. And if the above-average performance were the outcome of a value-added analysis, one would be unsure whether the school's performance was truly above average or whether it reflected bias in the model. To some extent, concerns about the bias in value-added estimates can be addressed by continuing research. However, since randomized experiments are rare in education—and those that are conducted take place in special circumstances so that generalizability can be a problem—it will be hard to ever be fully confident that the application of a particular statistical model in a specific setting produces essentially unbiased value-added estimates. Moreover, precision is an ongoing problem and, as Linn pointed out, there is a great deal of measurement error in the test results fed into these models, which in turn induces substantial uncertainty in the resulting estimates.

Any evaluation method leads to implicit causal interpretations. When a school does not make adequate yearly progress under the status model of No Child Left Behind, most people infer that this is an indication of the school's lack of effectiveness. With a little reflection, however, many will come to understand that a school serving a disadvantaged community faces a greater challenge in making adequate yearly progress than does a school serving an advantaged community. That is, many people understand that there are limits to what can be inferred from status results. Because value-added models involve sophisticated statistical machinery and the results explicitly attribute components of achievement gains to certain schools or teachers, people are more likely to accept the causal interpretations. The sources of imprecision and bias are less transparent but still present. Linn talked about the "scientific aura" around these models and the danger that it may lead people to place more faith in the results than is warranted.

Although none of the workshop participants argued against the possible utility of value-added modeling, there was a range of perspectives about its appropriate uses at this time. The most conservative perspective expressed at the workshop was that the models have more problems than current status measures and are appropriate only for low-stakes purposes, such as research. Others felt that the models would provide additional relevant information about school, teacher, or program effectiveness and could be employed in combination with other indicators. For example, many suggested that they could be useful in conjunction with status models to identify high and low performers. Still others argued that while the models have flaws, they represent an improvement compared with current practices—namely, status models for determining school performance under No Child Left Behind or credential-based promotion and rewards for teachers.

In sum, most of the workshop participants were quite positive about the potential utility of value-added models for low-stakes purposes, but much more cautious about their use for high-stakes decisions. Most agreed that value-added indicators might be tried out in high-stakes contexts, as long as the value-added information is one of multiple indicators used for decision making and the program is pilot-tested first, implemented with sufficient communication and training, includes well-developed evaluation plans, and provides an option to discontinue the program if it appears to be doing a disservice to educators or students.

References

Aaronson, D., Barrow, L., and Sanders, W. (2007). Teachers and student achievement in the Chicago public schools. *Journal of Labor Economics, 25*, 95-135.

American Educational Research Association, American Psychological Association, and National Council on Measurement in Education. (1999). *Standards for educational and psychological testing*. Washington, DC: Authors.

Ballou, D. (2005). Value-added assessment: Lessons from Tennessee. In R.W. Lissitz (Ed.), *Value-added models in education: Theory and application* (pp. 272-297). Maple Grove, MN: JAM Press.

Ballou, D. (2008). *Value-added analysis: Issues in the economics literature*. Paper prepared for the workshop of the Committee on Value-Added Methodology for Instructional Improvement, Program Evaluation, and Educational Accountability, National Research Council, Washington, DC, November 13-14. Available: http://www7.nationalacademies.org/bota/VAM_Workshop_Agenda.html.

Ballou, D., Sanders, W., and Wright, P. (2004). Controlling for student background in value-added assessment of teachers. *Journal of Educational and Behavioral Statistics, 29*(1), 37-65.

Braun, H. (2005). *Using student progress to evaluate teachers: A primer to value-added models*. Princeton, NJ: Educational Testing Service.

Brennan, R.L., Yin, P., and Kane, M.T. (2003). Methodology for examining the reliability of group difference scores. *Journal of Educational Measurement, 40*, 207-230.

Briggs, D. (2008). *The goals and uses of value-added models*. Paper prepared for the workshop of the Committee on Value-Added Methodology for Instructional Improvement, Program Evaluation, and Educational Accountability, National Research Council, Washington, DC, November 13-14. Available: http://www7.nationalacademies.org/bota/VAM_Workshop_Agenda.html.

Briggs, D.C., Weeks, J.P., and Wiley, E. (2008). *The sensitivity of value-added modeling to the creation of a vertical score scale*. Paper presented at the National Conference on Value-Added Modeling, University of Wisconsin-Madison, April 22-24.

California State Board of Education. (1997). *Mathematics content standards for California public schools, kindergarten through grade twelve.* Sacramento: California Department of Education. Available: http://www.cde.ca.gov/be/st/ss/documents/mathstandard.pdf [accessed January 2009].

Center for Educator Compensation Reform. (no date). *Teacher incentive grantee profiles.* Available: http://cecr.ed.gov/initiatives/grantees/profiles.cfm [accessed January 2009].

Clotfelter, C.T., Ladd, H.F., and Vigdor, J.L. (2007). *Teacher credentials and student achievement in high school: A cross-subject analysis with student fixed effects.* Working paper 13617. Cambridge, MA: National Bureau of Economic Research.

Easton, J. (2008). *Goals and aims of value-added modeling: A Chicago perspective.* Paper prepared for the workshop of the Committee on Value-Added Methodology for Instructional Improvement, Program Evaluation, and Educational Accountability, National Research Council, Washington, DC, November 13-14. Available: http://www7.national academies.org/bota/VAM_Workshop_Agenda.html.

Graham, S.E., Singer, J.D. and Willett, J.B. (in press). Longitudinal data analysis. In A. Maydeu-Olivares and R. Millsap (Eds.), *Handbook of quantitative methods in psychology.* Thousand Oaks, CA: Sage.

Hanushek, E. (1972). *Education and race.* Lexington, MA: D.C. Heath and Company.

Harris, D.N., and Sass, T. (2005). *Value-added models and the measurement of teacher quality.* Paper presented at the annual conference of the American Education Finance Association, Louisville, KY, March 17-19.

Holland, P. (2002). Two measures of change in gaps between the CDFs of test score distributions. *Journal of Educational and Behavioral Statistics, 27*(1), 3-17.

Isenberg, E. (2008). *Measuring teacher effectiveness in Memphis.* Washington, DC: Mathematica Policy Research.

Jha, A.K. (2008). *The impact of public reporting of quality of care: Two decades of U.S. experience.* Paper prepared for the workshop of the Committee on Value-Added Methodology for Instructional Improvement, Program Evaluation, and Educational Accountability, National Research Council, Washington, DC, November 13-14. Available: http://www7. nationalacademies.org/bota/VAM_Workshop_Agenda.html.

Koedel, C., and Betts, J. (2009). *Value-added to what? How a ceiling in the testing instrument influences value-added estimation.* Available: http://economics.missouri.edu/working-papers/koedelWP.shtml [accessed September 2009].

Ladd, H.F. (2008). *Discussion of papers by Dale Ballou and by Daniel McCaffrey and J.R. Lockwood.* Paper prepared for the workshop of the Committee on Value-Added Methodology for Instructional Improvement, Program Evaluation, and Educational Accountability, National Research Council, Washington, DC, November 13-14. Available: http://www7. nationalacademies.org/bota/VAM_Workshop_Agenda.html.

Linn, R.L. (1993). Linking results of district assessments. *Applied Measurement in Education, 6,* 83-102.

Linn, R.L. (2008). *Measurement issues associated with value-added models.* Paper prepared for the workshop of the Committee on Value-Added Methodology for Instructional Improvement, Program Evaluation, and Educational Accountability, National Research Council, Washington, DC, November 13-14. Available: http://www7.nationalacademies.org/ bota/VAM_Workshop_Agenda.html.

Lockwood, J.R., and McCaffrey, D.F. (2007). Controlling for individual heterogeneity in longitudinal models, with applications to student achievement. *Electronic Journal of Statistics, 1,* 223-252 (electronic). DOI: 10.1214/07-EJS057.

Lockwood, J.R., McCaffrey, D.F., Hamilton, L.S., Stecher, B.M., Le, V., and Martinez F. (2007). The sensitivity of value-added teacher effect estimates to different mathematics achievement measures. *Journal of Educational Measurement, 44*(1) 47-67.

Martineau, J.A. (2006). Distorting value-added: The use of longitudinal, vertically scaled student achievement data for growth-based, value-added accountability. *Journal of Educational and Behavioral Statistics, 31*(1), 35-62.

McCaffrey, D., and Lockwood, J.R. (2008). *Value-added models: Analytic issues.* Paper prepared for the workshop of the Committee on Value-Added Methodology for Instructional Improvement, Program Evaluation, and Educational Accountability, National Research Council, Washington, DC, November 13-14. Available: http://www7.national academies.org/bota/VAM_Workshop_Agenda.html.

McCaffrey, D., Lockwood, J.R., Koretz, D.M., and Hamilton, L.S. (2003). *Evaluating value-added models for teacher accountability.* Santa Monica, CA: RAND Corporation.

McCaffrey, D., Sass, T.R., and Lockwood, J.R. (2008). *The intertemporal effect estimates.* Paper presented at the National Conference on Value-Added Modeling, University of Wisconsin-Madison, April 22-24.

Mislevy, R.J. (1992). *Linking educational assessments: Concepts, issues and prospects.* Princeton, NJ: Educational Testing Service.

Murnane, R.J. (1975). *The impact of school resources on the learning of inner city children.* Cambridge, MA: Ballinger.

National Research Council. (1999). *High stakes: Testing for tracking, promotion, and graduation.* Committee on Appropriate Test Use. J.H. Heubert and R.M. Hauser (Eds.). Board on Testing and Assessment, Commission on Behavioral and Social Sciences and Education. Washington, DC: National Academy Press.

National Research Council. (2001). *Knowing what students know: The science and design of educational assessment.* Committee on the Foundations of Assessment, J. Pellegrino, N. Chudowsky, and R. Glaser (Eds.). Board on Testing and Assessment, Division of Behavioral and Social Sciences and Education. Washington, DC: National Academy Press.

National Research Council. (2005). *Systems for state science assessment.* Committee on Test Design for K-12 Science Achievement. M.R. Wilson and M.W. Bertenthal (Eds.). Center for Education, Division of Behavioral and Social Sciences and Education. Washington, DC: The National Academies Press.

National Research Council. (2007a). *Ready, set, SCIENCE!: Putting research to work in K-8 science classrooms.* S. Michaels, A.W. Shouse, and H. A. Schweingruber. Center for Education, Division of Behavioral and Social Sciences and Education. Washington, DC: The National Academies Press.

National Research Council. (2007b). *Taking science to school: Learning and teaching science in grades K-8.* Committee on Science Learning, Kindergarten through Eighth Grade. R.A. Duschl, H.A. Schweingruber, and A.W. Shouse (Eds.). Center for Education, Division of Behavioral and Social Sciences and Education. Washington, DC: The National Academies Press.

National Research Council. (in press). *Incentives and test-based accountability in public education.* Committee on Incentives and Test-Based Accountability in Public Education. M. Hout, N. Chudowsky, and S. W. Elliott (Eds.). Board on Testing and Assessment, Center for Education, Division of Behavioral and Social Sciences and Education. Washington, DC: The National Academies Press.

Organisation for Economic Co-operation and Development. (2008). *Measuring improvements in learning outcomes: Best practices to assess the value-added of schools.* Paris: Author.

Popham, W.J. (2007). Instructional insensitivity of tests: Accountability's dire drawback. *Phi Delta Kappan, 89*(2), 146-150.

Public Impact/Thomas B. Fordham Institute. (2008). *Ohio value-added primer: A user's guide.* Washington, DC: Thomas B. Fordham Institute. Available: http://www.edexcellence. net/doc/Ohio_Value_Added_Primer_FINAL_small.pdf [accessed January 2009].

Reardon, S., and Raudenbush, S.W. (2008). *Assumptions of value-added models for measuring school effects.* Presented at the Conference on Value-Added Modeling, University of Wisconsin-Madison, April 22-24.

Reckase, M.D. (2008). *Measurement issues associated with value-added models.* Paper prepared for the workshop of the Committee on Value-Added Methodology for Instructional Improvement, Program Evaluation, and Educational Accountability, National Research Council, Washington, DC, November 13-14. Available: http://www7.national academies.org/bota/VAM_Workshop_Agenda.html.

Rogosa, D.R., and Willett, J.B. (1983). Demonstrating the reliability of the difference score in the measurement of change. *Journal of Educational Measurement, 20,* 335-343.

Rothstein, J. (2009). *Student sorting and bias in value-added estimation: Selection on observables and unobservables.* Working Paper No. w14666. Cambridge, MA: National Bureau of Economic Research.

Sanders, W., and Horn, S. (1998). Research findings from the Tennessee value-added assessment system (TVAAS) database: Implications for educational evaluation and research. *Journal of Personnel Evaluation in Education, 12*(3), 247-256.

Sanders, W., and Rivers, J. (1996). *Cumulative and residual effects of teachers on future student academic achievement.* Knoxville: University of Tennessee Value-Added Assessment Center. Available: http://www.cgp.upenn.edu/pdf/Sanders_Rivers-TVASS_teacher%20effects.pdf [accessed June 2009].

Schmidt, W.H., Houang, R.T., and McKnight, C.C. (2005). Value-added research: Right idea but wrong solution? In R. Lissitz (Ed.), *Value-added models in education: Theory and applications* (Chapter 6). Maple Grove, MN: JAM Press.

Tong, Y., and Kolen, M.J. (2007). Comparisons of methodologies and results in vertical scaling for educational achievement tests. *Applied Measurement in Education, 20*(2), 227-253.

U.S. Department of Education. (2009, January 12). *Growth models: Non-regulatory guidance.* Washington, DC: Author. Available: http://www.ed.gov/admins/lead/account/growthmodel/index.html [accessed June 2009].

Willett, J.B., and Singer, J.D. (in preparation). *Applied multilevel data analysis.* Harvard University, Cambridge, MA.

Willms, J.D. (2008). *Seven key issues for assessing "value-added" in education.* Paper prepared for the workshop of the Committee on Value-Added Methodology for Instructional Improvement, Program Evaluation, and Educational Accountability, National Research Council, Washington, DC, November 13-14. Available: http://www7.national academies.org/bota/VAM_Workshop_Agenda.html.

Wright, S.P., Horn, S.P., and Sanders, W.L. (1997). Teacher and classroom context effects on student achievement: Implications for teacher evaluation. *Journal of Personnel Evaluation in Education, 1*(1), 57-67.

Xu, Z., Hannaway, J., and Taylor, C. (2007). *Making a difference? The effects of Teach For America in high school.* Washington, DC: Urban Institute. Available: http://www.urban.org/UploadedPDF/411642_Teach_America.pdf [accessed January 2009].

Young, M.J. (2006). Vertical scales. In S.M. Downing and T.M. Haladyna (Eds.), *Handbook of test development* (pp. 469-485). Mahwah, NJ: Lawrence Erlbaum Associates.

Zumbo, B.D., and Forer, B. (2008). *Testing and measurement from a multilevel view: Psychometrics and validation.* In J. Bovaird, K. Geisinger, and C. Buckendahl (Eds.), *High stakes testing in education: Science and practice in K-12 settings.* Washington, DC: American Psychological Association Press.

Zurawsky, C. (2004). Teachers matter: Evidence from value-added assessment. *Research Points: Essential Information for Educational Policy, 2*(2).

Appendix A

Workshop Agenda and Participants

Thursday, November 13, 2008, Lecture Room

10:00   **Welcome, Overview**
Stuart Elliott, Director, Board on Testing and Assessment
Henry Braun, Committee Chair

10:15   **Panel 1: Goals and Uses of VAM**
Moderator: Jane Hannaway
(20 minutes per presenter/discussant)

- Presentation by John Easton, Consortium on Chicago School Research
- Presentation by Derek Briggs, University of Colorado
- Discussion by Robert Gordon, Center for American Progress
- Discussion by Brian Stecher, RAND Corporation

Focused Discussion
Discussion Leaders: Henry Braun, Lorrie Shepard

12:15   **Working Lunch**
Continued discussion of the goals and uses of VAM

1:15   **Panel 2: Measurement Issues with VAM**
                Moderator: Mark Wilson

- Presentation by Mark Reckase, Michigan State
  University
- Presentation by Bob Linn, University of Colorado
- Discussion by Mike Kane, National Conference of
  Bar Examiners
- Discussion by Mike Kolen, University of Iowa

Focused Discussion
Discussion Leaders: Kevin Lang, Scott Marion

3:30   **Break**

3:45   **Focused Discussion (cont.)**

4:15   **Synthesis of Main Messages**
                Discussion Leader: Henry Braun

4:45   **Adjourn Workshop Day 1**

Friday, November 14, 2008, Lecture Room

OPEN SESSION

8:30   **Working Continental Breakfast**
                Prepare for discussion of analytic issues with VAM

9:00   **Welcome, Overview of the Day**
                Panel 3: Analytic Issues with VAM
                Moderator: Scott Marion

- Presentation by Dale Ballou, Vanderbilt University
- Presentation by Dan McCaffrey and J.R. Lockwood,
  RAND Corporation
- Discussion by Helen Ladd, Duke University
- Discussion by Sean Reardon, Stanford University

10:20   **Break**

10:35   Focused Discussion
                Discussion Leaders: Judy Singer, Mark Wilson

11:45   **Working Lunch**
Prepare for discussion of consequences of using VAM

12:45   **Panel 4: Short-Term and Long-Term Consequences**
Moderator: Judy Singer

- Presentation by Ashish Jha, Harvard School of Public Health
- Presentation by Doug Willms, University of New Brunswick
- Discussion by Adam Gamoran, University of Wisconsin–Madison
- Discussion by Ben Jensen, Organisation for Economic Co-operation and Development (OECD)

Focused Discussion
Discussion Leaders: Jane Hannaway, Lorrie Shepard

2:45   **Break**

3:00   **Synthesis of Main Messages**
Discussion Leader: Henry Braun

4:00   **Adjourn Workshop**

PARTICIPANTS

Rita Ahrens, Education Policy Studies
Joan Auchter, National Board for Professional Teaching Standards
Terri Baker, Center for Education, The National Academies
Dale Ballou, Vanderbilt University
Henry Braun, Boston College
Derek Briggs, University of Colorado at Boulder
Tom Broitman, National Board for Professional Teaching Standards
Alice Cain, House Committee on Education and Labor
Duncan Chaplin, Mathematica Policy Research
Naomi Chudowsky, Center for Education, The National Academies
Pat DeVito, AE Concepts
Beverly Donohue, New Visions for Public Schools
Karen Douglas, International Reading Association
Kelly Duncan, Center for Education, The National Academies
John Q. Easton, Consortium on Chicago School Research
Stuart W. Elliott, Center for Education, The National Academies

Maria Ferrão, Universidade da Beira Interior, Portugal
Rebecca Fitch, Office of Civil Rights
Shannon Fox, National Board for Professional Teaching Standards
Jianbin Fu, Educational Testing Service
Adam Gamoran, University of Wisconsin–Madison
Karen Golembeski, National Association for Learning Disabilities
Robert Gordon, Center for American Progress
Jeffrey Grigg, University of Wisconsin
Victoria Hammer, Department of Education
Jane Hannaway, Education Policy Center
Patricia Harvey, Center for Education, The National Academies
Lloyd Horwich, House Committee on Education and Labor
Lindsey Hunsicker, Committee on Health, Education, Labor, and
    Pensions
Ben Jensen, Organisation for Economic Co-operation and Development
Ashish Jha, Harvard School of Public Health
Moshe Justman, Ben Gurion University, Israel
Laura Kaloi, National Association for Learning Disabilities
Michael Kane, National Conference of Bar Examiners
Judith Koenig, Center for Education, The National Academies
Michael J. Kolen, University of Iowa
Adam Korobow, LMI Research Institute
Helen F. Ladd, Duke University
Kevin Lang, Boston University
Sharon Lewis, House Committee on Education and Labor
Valerie Link, Educational Testing Service
Dane Linn, National Governors Association
Robert L. Linn, University of Colorado at Boulder
J.R. Lockwood, RAND Corporation
Angela Mannici, American Federation of Teachers
Scott Marion, National Center for the Improvement of Educational
    Assessment
Daniel F. McCaffrey, RAND Corporation
Alexis Miller, LMI Research Institute
Raegen Miller, Center for American Progress
John Papay, Harvard University
Liz Potamites, Mathematica Policy Research
Ali Protik, Mathematica Policy Research
Sean Reardon, Stanford University
Mark D. Reckase, Michigan State University
Andre Rupp, University of Maryland
Sheila Schultz, HumRRO
Lorrie Shepard, University of Colorado at Boulder

Judith Singer, Harvard University
Andrea Solarz, Director of Research Initiatives, National Academy of
    Education
Gerald Sroufe, American Educational Research Association
Brian Stecher, RAND Corporation
Justin Stone, American Federation of Teachers
David Wakelyn, National Governors Association
Greg White, Executive Director, National Academy of Education
J. Douglas Willms, University of New Brunswick
Mark Wilson, University of California, Berkeley
Laurie Wise, HumRRO

Appendix B

Biographical Sketches of Committee Members and Staff

Henry Braun (*Chair*) holds the Boisi Chair in Education and Public Policy in the Lynch School of Education at Boston College. He also serves as distinguished presidential appointee (retired) at Educational Testing Service in Princeton, NJ. Among the more recent reports Braun authored or coauthored are *Exploring What Works in Science Instruction: A Look at the Eighth Grade Science Classroom* (2009), *America's Perfect Storm: Three Forces Changing our Nation's Future* (2007), and *A Closer Look at Charter Schools Using Hierarchical Linear Modeling* (2005). He has done considerable work in the area of value-added modeling and authored *Using Student Progress to Evaluate Teachers: A Primer on Value-Added Models* (2006). He was a program committee member for the 2008 conference on value-added modeling at the University of Wisconsin's Center for Education Research and a contributor the OECD monograph *Measuring Improvements in Learning Outcomes: Best Practices to Assess the Value-added of Schools* (2008). At the National Research Council, he is a member of the Committee on Incentives and Test–Based Accountability. He has a bachelor's degree in mathematics from McGill University and M.A. and Ph.D. degrees, both in mathematical statistics, from Stanford University.

Naomi Chudowsky (*Costudy Director*) has worked on a variety of studies at the National Research Council related to testing and accountability. These include reports on how incentives function in accountability systems, advances in the cognitive sciences and the implications for designing educational assessments, and the redesign of the U.S. naturalization tests.

She is also a consultant who conducts research on testing and accountability for state and national clients. She has researched and written a number of reports on the No Child Left Behind Act for the Center on Education Policy. Previously she worked on test development for President Clinton's Voluntary National Testing Initiative at the U.S. Department of Education and served as the coordinator of Connecticut's statewide high school testing program. She has a Ph.D. in educational psychology from Stanford University.

Stuart W. Elliott (*Senior Program Officer*) is director of the Board on Testing and Assessment at the National Research Council, where he has worked on a variety of projects related to assessment, accountability, teacher qualifications, and information technology. Previously, he worked as an economic consultant for several private-sector consulting firms. He was also a research fellow in cognitive psychology and economics at Carnegie Mellon University and a visiting scholar at the Russell Sage Foundation. He has a Ph.D. in economics from the Massachusetts Institute of Technology.

Jane Hannaway is the director of the Education Policy Center at the Urban Institute. She is an organizational sociologist whose work focuses on the study of educational organizations. Her areas of expertise include elementary and secondary schools, employment and education, school and teacher evaluations, standards-based reform, and vouchers. Her recent research focuses on structural reforms in education, particularly reforms promoting accountability, competition, and choice. She was recently appointed director of the Center for Analysis of Longitudinal Databases in Education Research (CALDER) at the Urban Institute. She is a past vice president of the American Educational Research Association and has served on its executive board. She was elected to the Council of the Association for Public Policy and Management. She is past editor of *Educational Evaluation and Policy Analysis*, the main policy journal of the American Educational Research Association. She is currently on the executive board of the American Education Finance Association. She has a Ph.D. in the sociology of education from Stanford University.

Judith A. Koenig (*Costudy Director*) is a senior program officer for the Board on Testing and Assessment. Since 1999, she has directed measurement-related studies designed to inform education policy, including studies on the National Assessment of Educational Progress, inclusion of special needs students in assessment programs, developing assessments for state and federal accountability programs, and setting standards for the National Assessment of Adult Literacy. From 1984 to 1999, she worked